PLANNING YOUR
college
education

By William A. Rubinfeld

vgm

Vocational Guidance Manuals
A Division of Data Courier, Inc.
Louisville, Kentucky

Copyright © 1964, 1976
Vocational Guidance Manuals, Inc.
A Division of
Data Courier, Inc.
620 South Fifth Street
Louisville, Kentucky 40202

Publisher—Loene Trubkin
Editor—Christine Maddox
Photo Editor—Donna Lawrence
Production Manager—Carmen Chetti
Production Supervisor—Sylvia Ward

Manufactured in the
United States of America

Revised edition

Library of Congress Catalog Card Number 76-5713

ISBN Number 0-89022-215-0 (Hardcover)
          0-89022-038-7 (Paperbound)

Cover photo by Toni Hoehle

To Ann,
My Right Hand.

ABOUT THE AUTHOR

Dr. William A. Rubinfeld, Coordinator of the Student Personnel Services training program in the Department of Foundations of Education, Jersey City State College since 1967, has been in the guidance field for the past 27 years. From 1948 to 1951, he was a part-time counselor at Barringer High School, Newark, New Jersey; from 1951 until 1960, he was head counselor at Weequahic High School, also in Newark. In 1960 he became director of guidance at Mountain High School, West Orange, New Jersey, and in 1965 he assumed the position of director of student personnel services for the city of West Orange. For the past ten years he has been practicing privately as an educational and vocational counselor. In this capacity he has counseled thousands of students regarding their educational planning, career selection, private school placement, college entrance problems, and graduate/professional school admissions.

Dr. Rubinfeld is affiliated with the following organizations: American Personnel and Guidance Association, National Vocational Guidance Association (professional membership), American School Counselor Assocation, American Psychological Association, New Jersey Psychological Association, New Jersey Personnel and Guidance Association, New Jersey Association of College Admissions Counselors, New Jersey Education Association, and Phi Delta Kappa, national honorary educational fraternity. He has been very active in the Association of College Admissions Counselors and has served as president of the New Jersey Chapter of that organization. Dr. Rubinfeld has had articles published in the *Personnel and Guidance Journal,*

Vocational Guidance Quarterly, School Counselor, The Bulletin of the National Association of Secondary School Principals, and *New Jersey Guidance News.*

The author received his B.A. degree from Washington Square College, New York University, and his Ed.D. degree from the School of Education, New York University. He also studied at Washington University, St. Louis, and at Rutgers University.

TABLE OF CONTENTS

Effects on earning capacity. Studies on earnings.
Pressures for an education. Who should go to college?
The boy down the street. Work and wait. Period-of-
work plus evening college. High school deficiencies.
Service enlistment. Remedial programs. Junior col-
leges and technical institutes.

Accelerated programs. Selection of languages. Mathematics requirements. Science requirements. General
requirements. College catalogs. Analyzing a catalog.
Admission requirements. Course offerings. Degree
programs. Other items of interest. Good study habits.
Extra- or co-curricular activities. Exploratory curricular experiences. Guidance and counseling services.
Library facilities. College and career conferences.
Visiting local schools. Part-time employment. Participation in sports. Other important activities.

Costs. All-male, all-female, or coed. Commuting vs.
living away from home. Distance and transportation
problems. Large vs. small college. Public, private, or
denominational schools. Course offerings. Accreditation—types, meaning, importance. Social levels of

college population. Academic levels. Urban, semi-urban, or rural setting. Location. Library. Ratio of students to faculty. Year-round campus. Attending schools outside your district. Geographical factors. Experimental programs and curricula.

anteed Student Loan Program. National Merit Scholarship Program. National Achievement Scholarship Program for Outstanding Negro Students. Other scholarship opportunities. State rehabilitation commissions. State and other scholarship help. Aid through professional organizations. Evaluating scholarship needs. Varying attitudes on need. "No need" scholarships. Effects of scholarship applications. Applying for a scholarship. Securing scholarship help. Helpful scholarship sources. Newspaper announcements. Local service clubs. Part-time employment in college. Allocating time for work.

INTRODUCTION

This book is an outgrowth of a guide originally prepared for parents of high school students. Our school had been conducting special evening programs for parents of juniors interested in attending college. After our talks, which presented the major considerations in selecting a college, the floor was opened to questions. The numerous and varied questions which followed the talks held our audiences far beyond the announced closing time, since they concerned problems of immediate interest. We retained the questions and then prepared a booklet with the answers to those questions which appeared to be of greatest concern. The circulation of this college guide stimulated interest for an expanded book written for both parents and students. A number of people mentioned that, despite the many excellent books which had been published on the vital subject of gaining admission to college, not one had been written by a person working directly with the problem in a high school—a high school guidance counselor who, because of his daily experience with the many and varied problems connected with college entrance, would be in an excellent position to be objective and to evaluate the situation realistically, from a broad viewpoint.

This book attempts to do the following: review the reasons for the desirability of a college education; suggest plans for those who aspire to college but whose achievement in high school has not been good; aid students in beginning to plan for college as early as the junior high school years; explore course selection in high school; and broadly outline methods of reading and using college catalogs. Emphasis also is placed on development of study habits and extracurricular and curricular experiences.

Students who read this book and follow its many suggestions will be more likely to choose a suitable school and make a better adjustment to college life than will those who pursue admissions haphazardly. The tendency on the part of young people to be unorganized and uninformed as they prepare to enter college results in many mistakes and creates problems that might easily be avoided. When you consider the amount of time to be expended in study (from one to eight years beyond high school) and the amount of money your parents will be investing (from a minimum of $400 to as much as $6,500 per year), you should recognize the need for deliberation and studied consideration in this matter. Follow-up studies on young people who have prepared carefully and painstakingly under proper guidance for selection of a school or an occupation strongly confirm the fact that such informed young people adjust far better than those who approach the future indifferently.

Despite the fact that gaining college admission is much easier than in the past because more schools have introduced open admissions policies, the need for detailed investigation of college is paradoxically greater. It is true that some schools are now granting admissions to those whom they might have rejected a few years ago; however, not all of these have lessened their academic demands on students. As a result, a percentage of students who end the year on probation or are dropped from the rolls are unwitting pawns in the game of "covering operating costs." The same students, properly placed, might have been more successful in less demanding situations or in schools where they were not at the bottom of the barrel academically.

We have some advice to offer parents who will be reading this book with the intention of assisting their offspring in gaining college admission: your involvement could be all to the good; however, problems do ensue when parents write for catalogs, fill out applications, and express all their biases in the process of giving "good, sound advice" to their children. On a number of occasions, I have chided parents who sat in on a college counseling session, took notes and made lists, then said, "I will write for the catalogs within twenty-four hours." When I point out to them that their offspring will be attending school and will be faced with many doubts and decisions without the parents in the immediate vicinity, they retreat, stating, "I really didn't intend to do any of the writing." If the parents don't retreat, they often contend that their young people would not go to college because they would never write for material or fill out applications. The latter is, of course, a very weak but possibly honest answer. If this is true, parents should allow their children to make plans other than college.

The sooner young people learn that certain things will be expected of them, the quicker they will pick up all the pieces and put them together. A little faith, added to withdrawal of extensive parental assistance, may temporarily add to the parents' anxiety but should eventually help develop a more responsible, capable, and dependable young college student.

It is the hope of the author that this book may usefully add to the material already published to assist young people with their future plans and may lead them to a wise choice of a college. The author hopes also that parents will find answers to many questions that have disturbed them and that the book itself may serve as a means of enabling parents to join with their children in planning for the future.

The masculine pronouns are being used in this book for succinctness and are intended to refer to both females and males.

CHAPTER 1

WHY GO TO COLLEGE?

Although most students want a college education for the obvious purpose of improving their chances for a better and more important job, other reasons extending beyond this include a desire to increase personal growth, to understand society and its values, to learn more about our culture, and to develop a deeper appreciation of environmental influences. Above all, we trust that your education will enable you to make greater contributions to your community and society and to be of greater service to your fellow man.

EFFECTS ON EARNING CAPACITY

For a long time, the records abounded with favorable statistics showing the greater earning power of those with increased education. The most recent estimates of average earnings by years of school completed were compiled by the Bureau of Census at the end of 1972. According to their studies, the average high school graduate will earn $100,000 more in his lifetime than the individual without a high school diploma; the average college graduate will earn from $175,000 to $200,000 more in his lifetime than the high school graduate. These increases, however, cannot be attributed solely to education; they pertain to the average and may have been affected by unusual abilities, motivation, area opportunities for employment, special skills, family background, and marriage.

In spite of these factors, there is ample evidence today to show that more and more employers are searching for college graduates and are using the diploma as a guide for promotions within their own organizations, just as a high school diploma was considered essential for employment in earlier decades by most large firms. The trend today is requirement of a college diploma as an entree into many business areas and opportunities.

As this book was being revised, a recession had made job placement difficult and some students considered withdrawing from school because of limited job opportunities or the prospect of accepting positions for which they were over-qualified as college graduates. Balancing this trend were unemployed young people returning to school to keep occupied and possibly to qualify for a well-paying position.

STUDIES ON EARNINGS

There are a number of studies which question the financial advantages of investment in college. A recent study by Dr. Nollen, a professor at Georgetown University, contended that there was a definite closing of the gap between earnings of high school and college graduates. In his statistics, Dr. Nollen showed that high school graduates, aged 25 to 34, earned $8,300 in 1970 and $9,400 in 1972. White male college graduates, aged 25 to 34, earned $11,100 in 1970 and $11,550 in 1972. Dr. Nollen concluded that over a lifetime, an investment in college will not be as economically sound as it was in the past.

Other research, done under the auspices of Harvard University and the Center for Policy Alternatives at Massachusetts Institute of Technology, noted that college graduates were losing some of their economic advantages over the less educated and also were discovering that an education was not necessarily a guarantee of upward social mobility. This study particularly emphasized the reduction of the differences in earnings between high school and college graduates from 1969 to 1973. Male workers with college degrees earned 53 percent more than their counterparts with four years of high school but by 1973, the difference was only 40 percent. Other startling statistics were concerned with the stationary level of professional and mangerial jobs from 1969 to 1974. What was most disconcerting was the fact that one-third of the male and two-thirds of the female graduates in the 1970s have had to accept positions unrelated to their college majors, compared with 10 percent of the men and 13 percent of the women in the early 1960s. Some of the explanations of the decline in the economic value of going to college, as well as the lessening appeal of college, relate these developments to economic conditions as well as shifting mores, making college less attractive to some youths. The study made some comments about the probable upturn in job prospects for graduates in the 1980s with the final note that while things will get better, a college degree will never again be as important as it was in the past.

One of the rebuttals to these comments, *Degree and What Else,* by Dr. Withey of the University of Michigan, insisted that enough research is available to support other figures. Dr. Withey and his colleagues contended that college graduates not only earn more than high school graduates, but have steadier employment throughout their working lives, lower unemployment rates, much longer vacations, and many fringe benefits. They also commented that college graduates were much more likely to find job satisfaction and to enjoy such other benefits as greater personal and family stability and far more active political and social lives.

Another group, the American Association of State Colleges and Universities, refused to accept the thesis that fewer high school graduates are now going to colleges because of the lower value of higher education. They contend that the drop in college enrollments from middle and working class families has been caused by rising tuition and other college costs.

PRESSURES FOR AN EDUCATION

In addition to the degree trend in employment, we are now finding ourselves in a situation where greater social and cultural demands are being made for a higher education. Some of these demands may be imaginary; but as long as parents and youngsters have such feelings, recognition must be given to this factor.

As a guidance counselor who has been subjected to some of these demands, my urge previously was to attempt to dissuade parents and youngsters from considering college education if they lacked the aptitude, the grades, or real academic motivation. However, I learned to realize that this is a problem which we must face realistically. Those attending college only because of outside pressures (social and cultural) should be willing to withdraw and pursue another educational route as soon as they discover that college is not the place for them.

The marginal student who is being carried by the college by being placed on probation repeatedly, or by being given summer school opportunities to make up failures or to pick up his grade point average has a need for strength in facing up to his predicament. I have seen young people carried in this way for several years, sometimes being permitted to stay in school until their senior year. The axe falls at this time, because it becomes almost impossible for such students to maintain the required 2.0 or C average for the awarding of the degree. The entire experience can be self-defeating, since most colleges will not consider a transfer for this marginal type of student.

WHO SHOULD GO TO COLLEGE?

There are different theories about who should go to college. Years ago, many counselors used the criterion of a minimum intelligence quotient (I.Q.) of 115 or SAT scores of 400, and there were others who were of the opinion that an even higher I.Q. should be required. Today, many of us prefer not to use numerical values by themselves, since high school test scores may be inaccurate, and there are some students whose academic development is delayed until they are older.

An experience I had is worthwhile repeating. A veteran who was referred to me for career counseling had a transcript which ranked him 224th in a class of 225 and listed three I.Q.'s ranging from 92 to 95. As I spoke to him, I noted that he was very articulate, had a good vocabulary, and gave other indications of having academic potential. I administered an individual I.Q. on which he received a total scale of 115. This later score was far more indicative of his potential and, quite possibly, even did not do him complete justice. As he recounted his previous academic history, he spoke of being criticized by teachers and judged as a limited individual. He fulfilled their estimation of his capabilities by being non-productive and avoiding involvement in school work and exams. So much for the slavish dependence on tests.

Some scores may be disputed, particularly with reference to the culturally deprived or individuals with certain ethnic backgrounds. Fortunately, the drop in college enrollments has resulted in less emphasis on test scores, with a few schools stating that SAT's or ACT's need not be submitted.

Many counselors generally believe that anyone who has maintained an above-average record in a fairly competitive high school should, if interested, consider a higher education. Among this group of students will be the talented, the gifted, and the above-average. Those of average ability who have been willing to extend themselves in achieving academic success also might seriously consider college. We cannot, and should not, object to any youngster of average ability continuing his education if he is willing to utilize his aptitudes to their fullest and is eager for a higher education. Actually, two-year colleges offering one- or two-year training programs are particularly interested in working with the dedicated average student.

The door also should be left open for a youngster who has not adjusted well in high school but has given indication of academic potential through promising test results and occasional academic achievement. One of my most exciting educational experiences involved working with World War II veterans who returned to secondary schools after their discharge from service. Their academic successes were monumental; the vast majority went on to college, and many became professionals. A perusal of their original high school transcripts would have led to prognoses of guaranteed failure; a review of their behavior—cutting of classes, truancy, tardiness, lack of application, restlessness, and rebelliousness would also not have augured well for their eventual adjustment.

In most cases, the best criterion is still the school record. It is important, however, to evaluate this in context, since an above-average record is meaningless in a school with students of limited potential, inadequate staff, and a lack of facilities and equipment for proper training. For students from that background, a little more reliance should be placed on test scores than on academic achievement. If there are any doubts about an individual taking post-high school training, the decision should always be in favor of the student's desires.

THE BOY DOWN THE STREET

Many parents of children who have not done well in school tend to minimize poor records. Their conversations instead center around the assured eventual change once we have assisted their children in gaining admission to college. Their predictions are based on the oft-told tale of a boy who on a number of occasions was thrown out of school, did very poor academic work, ranked in the bottom quarter of his class, and finally was graduated by the skin of his teeth. The tale goes on to narrate the sudden change that took place in the boy after his first year of college and his eventual success—professionally, academically, and monetarily.

These are wonderful straws for parents, and in some instances, they are based on true situations. The only flaw in this argument is that it is predicated on the assumption that their youngsters have the same potential and drive as the one in the success story.

Counselors have sent many such students directly to college after high school. Unfortunately, many of them, lacking potential, good study habits, and a real desire for an education, soon find themselves failing. They return home in quest of a career and some other answer to their needs. Failure statistics for low-achievement individuals are much lower for veterans and others who took some time off after high school to pursue other activities before continuing their education.

WORK AND WAIT

Today, many young people take a year off after graduation from high school. Some of these are good students who feel they need to "find themselves" or to develop their identity. For those who have organized plans, the experience can be a very positive one; but for those who plan to use the time wandering and working only part-time, there is reason to question whether the experiences will have a maturing effect on them. Perhaps a wiser choice might be to attend college for a year or two, then to take some time off for travel or study abroad.

PERIOD-OF-WORK PLUS EVENING COLLEGE

Another answer for the student who professes a desire for an education, or whose parents are projecting one for him, is to start to lay a solid foundation for future education. This may be done in a number of ways. In large cities which offer postgraduate programs or evening high school courses, consideration might be given to this type of training.

Such programs may help a student make up missing units for college admission or may be a means of bettering his grades. Most importantly, they may become the bridge for the development of good study habits and proper techniques of school work, which are essential for proving readiness for a real college education.

One of the advantages of participating in evening college programs is that their admission requirements in many cases are not stringent; the experience may also give an indication of the student's ability to complete a higher education. Many evening colleges allow students to transfer to a regular day program, and other colleges will give more consideration to the marginal high school student who offers this type of training as further evidence of his readiness for college work.

HIGH SCHOOL DEFICIENCIES

For those who have equivalency diplomas, are ready to graduate from high school, or have graduated and suddenly find the need for additional units in order to gain entrance into college, deficiencies might be made up by attendance in evening high school programs, or by taking postgraduate work in the school from which they have graduated. Many counselors object to the latter because it is much easier for these students to fall back into their old habits if they remain in their former setting. It is far more advantageous to consider the evening high school programs, if available, since the students attending these schools generally are mature and well motivated to continue their education.

In addition, if money is available, one might consider attending a private preparatory school. Admission to the better private preparatory schools is no longer difficult, and prospective students can be more selective than in the past. A number of the accredited private schools at one time insisted that students enter in their junior year and remain for two years. Now there are very few preparatory schools that will not consider a post-graduate student.

One should be cautious about entering a nonaccredited preparatory school or taking correspondence courses. Although these may have value individually, a few schools or colleges may question their value or flatly refuse to grant credit for this work. The wisest approach to this specialized type of education is to write to a number of colleges which you are considering to secure their reaction to this type of post-high school educational program.

SERVICE ENLISTMENT

For high school graduates who are at a loss about their futures, consideration may be given to a service enlistment. The various services have many different programs, some of which will guarantee schooling and specialized training. There also has evolved a method of granting college credit for basic training, schooling, and specialized instruction. Several service programs make arrangements for college classes, either through attendance or via correspondence courses. One of the valid reasons for considering a service hitch is that there is a good possibility it may help mature those who have been unable to "find themselves" in high school.

At different times there have been G.I. bills which could assure a needy individual of financial assistance in defraying the cost of his education. If you are considering the service for this reason be certain to check the status of this type of aid. Educational assistance programs undergo frequent change, and your local Veterans Administration can give you the most current information.

If you are interested in the armed services and visit your local recruiting offices for information on the various programs, keep in mind that some of the enlistment personnel might oversell their own branch of service. Also recognize that once you take the oath of allegiance to serve your country, you may, if war breaks out, have a commitment that extends far beyond the planned time in service.

REMEDIAL PROGRAMS

Where there is uncertainty about the reasons for a poor high school record, and the school system maintains and supports a full-fledged counseling and diagnostic program, parents and students should use these services to the greatest extent possible. In this way, one may discover the causes for the deficiencies and possible solutions. Where these services are not available, consideration should be given to securing bona-fide professional help by arranging for diagnostic tests.

In securing assistance for students, it is extremely important that parents check thoroughly the professional status of the individual, agency, or group offering help. Your community or State Psychological Association will offer a listing of its professionally accredited members; and the International Association of Counseling Services (a board created by the American Personnel & Guidance Association), located at 1607 New Hampshire Avenue N.W., Washington, D.C. 20009, has a directory of approved counseling agencies and institutions throughout the country.

If such deficiencies as reading disabilities are discovered efforts should be made to correct these before a student continues his education. It is wise to have the remedial program parallel the educational program.

Some thought might also be given to techniques-of-study programs and courses now being offered by many junior colleges, colleges, and universities. These are particularly appropriate for persons who have never learned how to apply themselves properly and need the aid and guidance of individuals who are equipped to help. The best sources for this type of aid, whether they be reading or study programs, are your local schools or universities. You should be alert to the host of new reading centers now coming into existence which are profiting by the added attention being paid to educational disabilities. Some of the enterprises are bonafide, legitimate, and worthwhile; their claims can easily be verified by checking their credentials and then rechecking through college and university references. There are others that promise the world but are poorly staffed and ill-equipped to do a professional job.

The speedreading concerns resort to hard sell and charge exhorbitant fees. In checking with professional reading specialists, most indicate that speedreading success is quite deceptive; that in order to maintain the newly accomplished rate of speed, individuals must exercise or train every day, just as athletes must dedicate themselves in order to maintain their abilities. Most specialists seriously question the effectiveness of speedreading when compared to assistance with reading comprehension.

JUNIOR COLLEGES AND TECHNICAL INSTITUTES

One other solution for the student who has not performed well in high school is consideration of a two-year community college, private junior college, or two-year technical institute. Most of the two-year technical institutes combine college and technical training. The junior colleges, with very few exceptions, are willing to work with those students who enter with academic handicaps. A number of the two-year colleges arrange special programs, including remedial work in specific areas, reading programs, and study technique training, as well as pre-college programs which permit students to condition themselves to collegiate experiences as well as make up units to qualify for specialized programs.

Incidentally, many colleges have adapted their programs to the needs of students with deficiencies and will admit students on a conditional basis, with the understanding that they first undergo the remedial program while taking only a limited number of college courses. Once such students have completed the remedial program and have indicated by their grades in a few college courses that they are ready for a full program, they are then permitted to matriculate. Information about specialized programs to assist marginal students can be obtained by checking catalogs or by dropping notes to different two-year schools.

The technical institutes may be an excellent answer for the poor student who has a desire to continue his education and whose habits and instincts are decidedly along technical and mechanical lines. *Lovejoy's College Guide; Barron's Guide to the Two Year Colleges;* Cass & Birnbaum's *Comparative Guide to Junior and Two-Year Community Colleges;* the Department of Health, Education, and Welfare's *Associate Degrees and Other Formal Awards Below the Baccalaureate;* and Chronicle Guidance's *Guide to Two-Year College Majors and Careers* would readily supply information about such institutes. The latter two are most reliable, since they update their information more frequently than any of the other directories. The *Guide to Two-Year Majors and Careers* is generally available in your guidance office, or it can be purchased by writing directly to Chronicle Guidance, Moravia, New York 13118. The government publication, generally revised each year, may be purchased from the Superintendent of Documents, Washington, D.C. 20402.

CHAPTER 2

PREPARATION FOR COLLEGE

More and more, the eighth grade is becoming the year of decision for practically all students, since this is the time they must begin to plan their studies for the next year and possibly the ensuing four years. Some schools have no such problem because of their limited resources; their students take a college preparatory, general, business, secretarial, or technical program, with prescribed courses for each area. The trend today, however, is away from this type of programming to an individual guide for each student in terms of his plans and abilities.

Where courses are prescribed and facilities limited, students have no choice beyond selecting their field of interest—college, technical vocational training, or commercial schooling. In schools where courses are geared to the individual, the planning can become personalized, aiding considerably in better adjustment in high school and easier admission to college.

It is not the simplest matter in the world to make the best decision at this time. Most students in the eighth grade have not selected careers, do not have a real awareness of the type of school they may prefer at a later date, and are not fully ready to determine what best fits their particular situation. When this problem presents itself it is best to review your grades and test scores for the previous years and prepare a temporary program based on your scholastic experiences up to this time.

For example, if you have had difficulty in arithmetic throughout grade school, and this deficiency has been confirmed by test scores and the judgment of your teachers, you might temporarily forego taking algebra. You might experiment either with general mathematics or business arithmetic. Again, if you have had trouble in English or language arts classes, you should recognize that this is a fairly good predictor of possible difficulty with foreign languages.

In both these situations, you might take a college preparatory program but omit the subjects that might prove too difficult for you. You could verify through the use of catalogs that there are institutions which will still grant you admission without these college units.

For those who have no disabilities, the decision revolves around the selection of a language and the question of the need for the general science course which is given on the freshman level in most high schools.

ACCELERATED PROGRAMS

Those with evident ability or those who have been in an accelerated program in the eighth grade (generally algebra and a language) must decide whether to continue with selective, demanding classes or return to the regular schedule. There are many pro's and con's to be considered in an accelerated schedule. Of importance to most students and their parents is whether participation in honors, accelerated, or advanced placement classes is considered in preparing class rank. This question is not of grave consequence if colleges are familiar with the competitive nature of the particular high school. However, one is never certain who will be handling a transcript, and a negative reaction to a low class rank may damage a student's admission chances. There are a few high school administrators who simply weight all subjects, whether specialized or honor classes, with the minor subjects and vocational and commercial courses. Practically all schools today

Preparation for college should begin with a carefully planned high school curriculum.

issue a special profile, with a description of the courses as well as a thumbnail sketch of the community and its population. Frequently this includes the distribution of I.Q.'s, ACT's, and SAT's, with the format for ranking students. I would urge students to request a copy of the prepared profile to help them in making any decision about specialized programs and their effect on college admissions.

It would be my recommendation that students who have the innate ability take advantage of any accelerated or specialized program at their school. Some young people have a need for competition, and certainly peer group relationships are easier to establish when one is placed with many other students of comparable academic levels. Most students admitted to the program will secure a better and stronger self-concept.

There are some disadvantages to consider in any type of advanced program. There are a few colleges that may not look at the profile and thus fail to appreciate the rigorous type of training some of these students have undergone. There are some state colleges that insist on specific class rank for out-of-state students and will do no weighting to differentiate between the student from a highly competitive setting and the student who may be from a school where only ten or twenty percent of the graduates continue their education beyond high school.

Occasionally there are misplacements in accelerated education because the faculty at some schools are impressed by "busy workers" who compensate for their lack of ability by devoting tremendous numbers of hours to their assignments. In an ideal situation, parents, students, and counselors should sit down and weigh all the evidence to arrive at as objective an estimate as possible of the student's ability to adapt to competitive classes. When a decision is made for shifting a student to the honors classes, it would be wise to have a trial period, with in-depth consultation after a short period. If the program is contra-indicated, the administration should acquiesce to a change of schedule.

SELECTION OF LANGUAGES

At meetings with parents, one of the typical questions centers around the problem of taking Latin in high school. Questions such as, "Is Latin required for medicine, law, veterinary medicine, nursing, pharmacy, etc.?" come up at every one of our parents' meetings, and the answer we give is a straightforward "no." This by no means implies that you should not take Latin. Where programs permit and there is interest in majoring in languages or in fields involving use of the English language, serious consideration should be given to taking Latin.

A rundown of catalogs shows an extremely small percentage of schools which would still like Latin. In almost all cases, this requirement would be waived today. Very few colleges insist upon Latin for acquiring a B.A. degree, and it is no longer a "must." We get many different opinions concerning the preferred languages, but a review of most high schools shows a heavier interest in French than in most other languages.

Spanish has now become an entree to many positions because of the influx of Hispanics from Puerto Rico, Cuba, and South America. In trying economic times, the prospective employee who is bilingual has, without a doubt, many more job opportunities.

For those going into graduate work, a coin might actually be tossed as to whether French or German is preferable. Some believe that German is preferred by technical schools, but the evidence is not conclusive. A few schools insist that their chemistry majors study German. There are a number of "better" schools of technology and engineering that do not at the present time *insist* upon a language but do indicate that they would prefer at least two years of a modern language. Those students who foresee the possibility of working for a Ph.D. should think in terms of preparation in two modern language fields. (One of these may be delayed until after reaching college.)

There are still a very few colleges which recommend two languages. This requirement may be satisfied either by a combination of three years of one and two of another, or a program of two and two. The need to meet this type of language requirement has diminished considerably, but if there is any indication that you may be interested in a highly competitive school, catalogs should be checked to verify this need. *A general recommendation today is that those students who take languages in school should make every effort to take three or four years of one language rather than divide their time between two languages. Students planning on scientific or technical training should consider German, Russian, and French in that order.*

Students interested in Italian, Russian, Hebrew, and any other language not commonly given throughout the United States have a problem. If they hope to secure a B.A. degree without taking another language, they should check carefully the language offerings at different colleges. They may have to take a new language if they do not pass a placement test in the language studied in high school. Most schools used to insist upon evidence of modern language proficiency for the awarding of the B.A. degree, but there has been a gradual diminution of this requirement.

Rather sadly have I observed the trend away from the study of languages, with a lessening of requirements and the discontinuance of the language requirement for a B.A. degree. In coming decades, intercontinental travel will increase, and with detente, added to the growth in international business and trade, there could be many advantages for the linguist. Not many Americans are bilingual, and in our travels we depend upon residents of other nations to rescue us languagewise. High school students should consider taking languages for cultural, economic, and social reasons, and as evidence of our acknowledgement of the importance of other nations.

MATHEMATICS REQUIREMENTS

At the present time mathematics entrance requirements vary considerably from school to school and program to program. A very few schools are still willing to accept business arithmetic or general mathematics, whereas others prefer as much as five years of mathematics.

Where schools of business administration were once less demanding, more and more now expect their students to take at least one year of calculus. With the use of computers, more highly sophisticated developments in applied mathematics, and the extension of mathematical and statistical concepts in many business areas, the rationale for more solid math backgrounds takes on added meaning.

Schools of education, especially in the elementary field, are not too exacting in this area. On the other hand, technology institutes and colleges of engineering prefer a minimum of three-and-one-half to four years of mathematics and will give more attention to those who have had advanced algebra in addition to solid geometry and trigonometry. A number of the colleges of engineering and related schools are asking for College Board Achievement Tests in advanced mathematics.

When offered, and if you have the aptitude, take advantage of any courses in statistics, probability, trigonometry, advanced mathematics, and calculus. As a rule of thumb, take as much math as you can (notwithstanding your career plans), since the uses of math will be extended, and you may find yourself at a disadvantage in having to take some elementary math courses to compete adequately with other students. For example, if you should decide at some later date to major in psychology, you will be expected to cope with at least one course in statistics. If you move into the field of economics, there is now much wider use of diagnostic predictions (econometrics) through mathematics. If you should eventually plan on graduate school, there are very few programs that will not expect you to be able to handle statistics for research purposes.

If you have little mathematical ability and have attempted to do something about it to no avail, look for the programs with little or no math or the special math courses offered for the non-math student.

SCIENCE REQUIREMENTS

Here again we run the gamut from some schools which will not specify any science requirements, to others that look for a minimum of two years of laboratory sciences (biology, physics, or chemistry). Remember, to study physics and chemistry, you should have satisfactory marks in mathematics. If you are considering a scientific career or an engineering career, you should expose yourself to as much science as possible. Many engineering schools are insisting on the presentation of physics and chemistry for admission purposes.

Job opportunities in the allied health fields have been steadily increasing, with greater competition for entrance into such programs as nursing, medical technology, physical therapy, occupational therapy, dental hygiene, and physician's assistant. Practically all of these programs require a number of science units and expect their trainees to have facility with the sciences. Taking these courses will not only serve the purpose of helping you gain admission to a college, but may also help you decide whether you are ready to become involved in occupations requiring a science background.

GENERAL REQUIREMENTS

Your major problem in selecting high school subjects is that at various times you may be considering applying to colleges with different entrance requirements.

The wisest approach to this problem is to take a minimum of three years of one modern language; a minimum of one year of algebra and one year of geometry; at least one laboratory science; four years of English; and one year of history, then fill in the other five units with other subjects—mathematics, science, social studies, or foreign language. A transcript with these units would meet the requirements of 90 to 95 percent of the colleges throughout the United States. For some of the highly competitive schools, it might be wiser to offer more mathematics, more science, and possibly an additional language.

Oddly enough, the more competitive or more prestigious colleges have greater resiliency and flexibility and will so state in their bulletins. Do not allow the omission of a specific required unit from your transcript to deter you from applying to a college—give the school an opportunity to make their own decision.

The choice of units suggested at the beginning of this section should be based on a very careful reading of the requirements of schools whose demands are not great. A word of caution: *Schools are constantly changing their requirements and adding to the academic units they seek. You have no assurance that, if you meet the college requirements listed in catalogs when you are in the ninth year in high school, the requirements will be the same four years later.*

COLLEGE CATALOGS

It is never too early to begin reading college catalogs, which may be obtained in a variety of ways. Colleges, in view of the cost of catalogs, would naturally prefer your using all available library facilities. In addition, you may borrow college catalogs from your school library or guidance office. If you write for catalogs, address your request to the Registrar or the Director of Admissions. When writing to a large university, give some indication of your particular interests, since some of the larger universities use individual catalogs for their different colleges.

ANALYZING A CATALOG

Throughout the years, students have maintained a respectable distance from college catalogs. Their objections stem from the difficulty of getting similar basic information for different schools. Additionally, the style of writing does not add interest to the reading of the catalog, and there have been innumerable complaints about the format, content, and scope of these books. Still, since the outlook for a uniform type of catalog for all colleges, with a standardized frame of reference, is not a possibility within the near future, you should learn how to skim through a catalog for the information you may need. At a later date you may have to concentrate and cull minor bits of information, particularly when preparing to visit a college.

You should be aware of the index at the end of the catalog and use this for referring to sections of immediate interest. You should pay close attention to the admission requirements, and if these are couched in general terms, you will either have to do your own interpretation or write to the college for elaboration.

ADMISSION REQUIREMENTS

If a college states that it *prefers* so many units in specific subject areas without *insisting* upon them, you would be wise to attempt to meet these preferred requirements. On the other hand, colleges have and will make exceptions to any stated requirements. You should, if possible, secure evidence in writing of these possible deviations.

COURSE OFFERINGS

In reviewing college programs, you should make it a practice to see what types of courses are offered and look for the number of teachers within a department. One of the mistakes some students make is attending a college with plans to major in political science, only to discover that there are only two or three professors in their field. If the professors are good, this is an advantage; where the opposite is true, it becomes a major disadvantage.

If you want some statistics on the number of graduates who have completed a major in a specific area, use the United States Department of Health, Education, and Welfare publication, *Earned Degrees Conferred, 19___ to 19___*. These reports, although they are published annually, come out three years after students have graduated. They can give you an excellent picture of the size of the different departments. One word of caution—the number of graduates with a major in a subject like French cannot be considered without paying attention to the size of the school. Seven graduates with a major in French at a school of 1,000 might well be a higher percentage than 25 graduates with a major of French in a school of 5,000.

We know some students who very shrewdly, in the process of selecting a college, have gone through catalogs of the colleges of their choice and listed the course offerings in their fields of interest. They then made comparisons and used the resulting list as one criterion for selection.

DEGREE PROGRAMS

Although not of major importance when selecting a college, it is worthwhile to realize that colleges, in granting degrees, have requirements both in terms of courses and grade averages. From school to school there may be additional requisites which must be met before graduation. In addition, most catalogs will lay out the four-year programs, specifying courses that are required, number of credit hours for each course, and the number of credit hours for elective courses. Students frequently ask about the meaning of credit hours. Simply stated, a three-credit-hour course meets three hours per week, and successful completion of the course results in the student receiving three credit hours toward his degree.

The number of required and elective courses naturally is not identical from school to school. If you have difficulty in certain prescribed subject areas, it is sometimes feasible to consider a program at a school that allows for greater leeway in selecting courses. Approaching elective courses wisely may afford you many exploratory experiences and alert you to career areas that you might never have considered.

OTHER ITEMS OF INTEREST

A number of colleges list all students by grade levels and include their home areas. Such a listing would enable anyone investigating a particular college to get an idea of the geographical distribution, the names of possible contacts living within his immediate vicinity, and a generalized picture of the makeup of the student population.

Some catalogs also include names and addresses of the members of their alumni association, with a breakdown for all different areas. These lists could be used for reference purposes, but you should realize that all alumni suffer from a very pleasant type of belief—namely, that their college is by far the best in the entire country.

Other items which should be interesting in checking a catalog are the list of scholarships offered by the school and means of securing them; specific rules and regulations, including curfew hour; rules about use of automobiles; etc. If the school is a denominational one, the chapel rules and specific religious course requirements should be checked carefully. References will also be found to job opportunities, placement services, and the availability of counseling services.

The task of reading a catalog is a difficult one. Concentrating on one or two catalogs will simplify the process for you; once a frame of reference has been gained, you can learn how to assemble information about the highlights. Beyond that there is no need to delve deeply unless you have a special interest in the college.

GOOD STUDY HABITS

Psychologists, counselors, and teachers have learned over the years that adolescents have tremendous flexibility and that this period is one of the best times to develop good habits. Experience has taught us that the brightest students are not necessarily the best students. One of the reasons for this discrepancy is that some of the brightest students have poor study habits, whereas some of those with limited potential have learned how to apply themselves diligently.

Junior and senior high school days are an ideal time to develop study techniques which should be enduring, and most teachers and schools devote a good deal of time to this problem. Professionally prepared study guides may also prove helpful. It is advantageous to accept the judgment of teachers or these study guides by following a steady and consistent pattern of study habits.

Students whom we are reluctant to recommend for college entrance, despite evidence of academic potential, are primarily those who have not learned to apply themselves in school. They frequently say that when they reach college they will turn over a new leaf, dig into their studies, and prove their worth and ability. Despite the sincerity of their intentions, this rarely happens. The intentions are honorable, but the execution is far from simple.

EXTRA- OR CO-CURRICULAR ACTIVITIES

The need for participation in curricular and extra-curricular activities is fairly well recognized by students and parents. Colleges are looking for the well-rounded student and are requesting evidence of wholesome participation in such activities. All applications have questions in this area, but the evaluation of these activities and the need for them will vary considerably.

Highly competitive colleges, in issuing their profiles, show the makeup of their freshman class by giving the percentage who have been class presidents, held office in the student council, edited school newspapers, managed athletic teams, participated in athletics, and have been active in community affairs. For the student considering one of these schools, there is a great need for evidence of success in some activity, with the exception of the very brilliant, dedicated scholars who would be accepted for their ability to add to the academic prestige of the school. Many other schools are appreciative of active membership in school organizations but would rarely use the lack of activities to withhold acceptance.

Junior high school is a good time to join clubs and participate actively in some of the available facilities of the school. It is much wiser to concentrate on a few activities and develop depth in them. This is preferable to over-activity and superficial participation merely for the sake of showing membership. Most college admissions officers are alert to this technique and are not impressed.

Placing college demands aside, you should, if possible, take advantage of the extracurricular offerings of your school system so that you may grow and develop in all respects. Sometimes the poise and maturity developed as a result of these activities pays bigger dividends than the actual education itself. Not to be overlooked are the excellent opportunities to make friends, to widen your contacts, and to learn how to function in a social and group setting. Innate leadership qualities may come to the fore, and the knack of making decisions may be strengthened by some of your experiences.

EXPLORATORY CURRICULAR EXPERIENCES

Beginning in junior high school, and for the rest of your high school days, you should use to your advantage all experiences in subject areas. Despite the emphasis on testing today, many counselors have strong opinions about the predictive nature of school subjects in determining possible future careers. The pitfall in using this technique, however, is that personalities of teachers may color your judgments. There are situations where you believe that you have a strong interest in a subject, when actually you become so impressed by the teacher that you confuse the two. On the other hand, there are times when you may develop an intensive dislike for a particular subject. This antipathy may be based on your reaction to the teacher.

Omitting the teacher-personality factor, your enjoyment of specific subject fields is an excellent way to determine plans for the future. Throughout your junior and senior high school days you should consider every experience in a subject area as an exploratory one. Pay close heed to your reactions, likes, dislikes, and successes with each field. Then consider career fields that require facility in those subjects of interest to you.

GUIDANCE AND COUNSELING SERVICES

A generation ago most high schools had one individual, generally a member of the administrative staff, who assumed responsibility for educational and vocational guidance within the school. Today, most school systems have developed well-planned and well-staffed guidance offices to assist young people with educational, vocational, and personal problems.

Even in those systems with the equivalent of one full-time counselor for every 250 youngsters, many fail to take advantage of the opportunity to seek out this type of professional help. Working as the head of a guidance program for 15 years, the author has discovered that there are always a very few students who are persistent and constantly visit the guidance office. The vast majority come in only for their routine interviews, which usually are conducted twice a year.

High school students would do well to recognize the maxim that "the squeaky wheel gets the grease." If you are in a school system which is inadequately staffed, your persistence in asking for assistance may induce overworked guidance personnel to request additional manpower.

Most counselors find that too few young people take advantage of all the available guidance aids. Despite pleas on the part of the counseling staff, despite notices about special meetings, despite well-advertised invitations to hear college representatives, there is always a percentage of students who go blithely on their way. At a much later date, these students express regret at their failure to participate in these counseling experiences.

Guidance colleges today are equipped with a wealth of material—books on careers, college catalogs, scholarship information, college guide books, and technical and specialized school bulletins. Some have free literature that may be taken at any time; others offer loan services for some of their materials. The student who has failed to use such guidance resources effectively has deprived himself of a principal aid in selecting a college.

LIBRARY FACILITIES

It seems almost superfluous to remind young people that there are library facilities within most schools, or within the community, and that these libraries abound with material which might prove extremely helpful in selecting both careers and a school for higher education.

Even in those communities where the facilities are limited, resourceful librarians will invariably find some means of offering assistance. In all my years in the educational field, I have yet to meet a librarian, either in a school or public library, who was not eager to assist in finding desired materials. Perhaps the librarians, along with the counselors, should adopt merchandising techniques and notify the world at large that libraries generally have available the catalogs of practically all colleges and junior colleges in the United States, as well as other related information in this area.

Visiting and utilizing your library is just as important as visiting your counselor's office. Incidentally, guidance personnel would be most appreciative if students first attempted to borrow catalogs and other material from libraries, which have the staff and organized methods of loaning material.

COLLEGE AND CAREER CONFERENCES

Because of the economic crunch and the shortage of students, private colleges are still sending representatives to visit high schools; indeed, there have been more of these representatives recently than in the past.

Most schools send notices to all junior and senior (and sometimes sophomore) homerooms inviting interested youngsters to attend college conferences. Some high schools wisely include a brief description of the college, its course offerings, its population, and its cost to help students determine their interest in this type of school. Where schools do not do this, you would be wise to visit your library or guidance office and skim through the college catalog to determine your need to attend a particular conference. Again, too few students take advantage of the visits by these college representatives. They afford excellent opportunities to get firsthand information about a school and also are very helpful in alerting you to questions you may later use in investigating other schools. You should make it a practice to check conference schedules periodically so you can consider attending these which are of interest to you. If you have any doubts, go anyway!

There has been an increase in college days, generally with several high schools in an area or all the schools in a county or political district combining their efforts. In addition, several groups of admissions officers, representing as many as 15 or 20 colleges, have been visiting different areas in the U.S., spending a few days in a geographical area and announcing their availability through school guidance officials, newspapers, and letters to prospective students. They generally make themselves available for individual interviews, either during the school day or after school hours.

The National Association of College Admissions Counselors has sponsored college fairs in various parts of the country. Several hundred college admissions officials participate in this venture, and it affords students an opportunity to meet individuals from every section of the country and come in contact with every conceivable type of collegiate institution. The calendar for this type of college fair can be secured by writing to the National Association of College Admissions Counselors, 9933 Lawler Avenue, Suite 500, Skokie, Illinois 60076.

There are also advantages to attending career conferences, since career speakers may mention colleges that offer good programs in their fields. Several years ago we conducted weekly career conferences with attendance on a voluntary basis. When we tabulated the attendance for each student upon graduation, we learned that over fifty percent had never taken advantage of one of these conferences, and only about five percent had attended over ten in two years.

In a recent study which we conducted, those who attended career and college conferences overwhelmingly requested that we conduct more. The respondents suggested that we develop an improved technique of bringing more students into these conferences if we hoped to be of greater assistance to young people in high school.

VISITING LOCAL SCHOOLS

Another excellent opportunity for becoming familiar with colleges, their offerings, and other important details is to take notice of the many invitations extended by numerous colleges within commuting distance of your local high school and then devote a Saturday or week-day afternoon to visiting some of the schools.

Colleges are eager to have students visit with them and see them in action, and rarely do they limit numbers. Participation in local college visits necessitates paying attention to the announcements, visiting the guidance office periodically to see what is available, and then making the necessary arrangements to go on one of these trips. A major advantage of this type of activity is that you are able to substitute a firsthand picture for a catalog description of facilities, buildings, grounds, etc.

PART-TIME EMPLOYMENT

Previously we mentioned the emphasis placed by colleges on extracurricular activities. Knowing this, parents often question us about the advisability of their youngsters giving up part-time jobs in order to build a record of participation in school activities.

Without being in a position to speak for all college admission officers, we believe, on the basis of statements made by a number of them in the past, that most respect the holding of a job and will waive the consideration of extracurricular activities. In other words, many are aware that financial need does exist and are still pleasantly old-fashioned enough to recognize that application to a job outside of school supplies good evidence of of basic stability. Every time that parents have raised this question with us, we have recommended unhesitatingly that their youngsters continue working if the financial need existed.

This is a good opportunity to remind young people that most application blanks ask about work history, and evidence of summer employment during your high school days will prove helpful. Menial jobs will merit as much attention, if not more, than a soft job created by parents, relatives, or friends of the family. Positions that are related to your possible future career are also respected.

PARTICIPATION IN SPORTS

Not too long ago, one of my friends asked me whether his son should continue playing football and baseball in high school because of the sacrifice of time involved. I told him emphatically that athletics opened more doors for college acceptance than any other type of school activity, and in many situations athletic records receive greater attention than academic records. This is a realistic viewpoint based on my experiences and those of fellow counselors. As soon as we have an exceptional athlete, the phone starts ringing and inquiries are made about the young person's personality, academic record, and college potential. If this student is that rare combination of scholar and athlete, all sorts of doors will open for him. For some of the less competitive schools, any record of athletic success adds immeasurably to the opportunity for college acceptance and to the possibility of scholarship help.

Parents are not to construe these statements as guarantees that their athletic youngster will gain admission or secure scholarships, but they can rest assured that the likelihood of such opportunities will be heightened a great deal by participation in an athletic program. In speaking to groups of parents at open public meetings, I have constantly mentioned the importance colleges attach to *exceptional* athletic prowess.

There is some merit and justification for colleges' interest in athletes. Considering the amount of time they devote to practice and the energy they expend in demanding contests, in addition to coping with regular academic schedules, one has to respect the dedication of student athletes. An interesting sidelight is the general improvement of athletes' grades during their sport season. Apparently the need for organization of time and the tightness of schedules compels most athletes to utilize every minute advantageously.

OTHER IMPORTANT ACTIVITIES

With all of the emphasis on athletics, colleges are also searching for young people who may help their schools achieve a proper balance in other areas. Believe it or not, there is a shortage of good bassoon players, oboists, and string instrumentalists at a number of schools; skill with any one of these instruments will prove very valuable in gaining admission. Some schools even suggest that the young person bring the instrument along on his visit in order to demonstrate his ability by playing for their orchestra conductor and some of the faculty members.

There is also a desire on the part of colleges to attract young people who have indicated by their activities that they have qualities of leadership. As a result, a student holding office in the student council, maintaining membership in the student council, representing the school in youth sessions, either on a state or city level, or holding class office is regarded highly by college admissions committees.

Some students who hold office in national fraternities and religious organizations are given preference for admission by some of the prestigious colleges. Achievements in scouting are also looked upon with favor by admissions officers.

Hobbies of all sorts add to a college applicant's attractiveness. What is most impressive is serious, consistent, and meaningful involvement, plus the obvious knowledge associated with the specific hobby. Superficiality is not respected—you may encounter interviewers who are sophisticated and very knowledgeable about your chosen hobby. They may ask penetrating questions.

CHAPTER 3

SELECTING A COLLEGE

Selecting the proper college is not an easy task, and choosing the wrong one can be disappointing, and perhaps even disastrous, to a young person's educational development. There are several criteria by which schools can be judged, and careful evaluation of the following should help assure students and their parents that they have chosen the right one.

COSTS

Realistically speaking, although costs should not be the major factor, it is wise to take them into consideration before applying other criteria in the selection of a college.

We always recommend that students sit down with their parents when they are ready to give serious consideration to selection of a school and work out a financial statement which should reveal, within one or two hundred dollars, the amount available from the family and other sources. This procedure should include the student's savings, an approximation of possible summer earnings, and income from other employment sources. It should enable most families to decide tentatively on the type of school they can afford and may be a strong determinant in college selection.

Since state universities, state colleges, and some municipal colleges generally offer the lowest tuition rates (in some counties and municipalities tuition is free), students with limited incomes should investigate the possibility of acceptance at one of these institutions.

When private colleges are considered, the costs naturally are much greater. Despite the fact that these institutions are nonprofit organizations, they must supplement the tuition received with endowments and gifts from alumni. The most expensive schools have tuition rates from $4,000 to $4,500 a year and board expenses varying from $1,500 to $2,500 a year. Since these charges may vary, it would be wise to check catalogs periodically for any changes.

Above and beyond tuition and board, you must consider other fees, which may run as high as $1,000. Cost of books, clothing, pocket money for entertainment purposes, and transportation must be included in your estimate. The cost of books may be kept down by purchasing secondhand books or using the reference textbooks available in the college library.

Clothing costs do not have to be prohibitive, since today's styles call for male and female students to wear jeans, sport or work shirts, and mocassins or sandals. Even at costly schools, there does not appear to be a competitive situation in wearing apparel, but some thought has to be given to clothing in estimating college expenses.

Transportation costs may be a large item in a student's budget, since most people hope to return home during the academic year, at least during Christmas and Easter holidays. This may be one reason why so many students prefer colleges within 200 or 250 miles of their homes. On the other hand, some students who attend distant schools cut down transportation costs by sharing travel expenses in a fellow student's car. For those who prefer flying and getting home more often, costs may be rather extensive, and budget provisions should be made for such preferences.

What is important to realize is that there are a number of hidden costs which should be taken into consideration in making financial plans for an education. Additionally, to whatever figures are offered in a college catalog, it is expedient to add $300 to $500 to cover unforeseen expenditures.

Another section of this book will elaborate on other means of realistically appraising the family income in order to finance an education.

ALL-MALE, ALL-FEMALE, or COED

Most psychologists would readily dispose of this problem by stating that it is better for students to secure an education in a normal setting, and having the two sexes together is by far the more natural. Those who argue for the coeducational viewpoint offer this argument, plus the fact that coed classes enable you to receive both the male and female point of view. Coed schooling also prepares both sexes for community living and getting along with other people. Some contend that since most young people come from a coeducational high school, the coed situation on a college level is a normal follow-up.

On the other hand, there are those who argue for schools admitting only one sex. These advocates contend that there are greater opportunities for self-expression and for better career preparation at such institutions. A great deal of material has been published arguing that there is much higher academic achievement in schools whose student populations are all male or all female. This is borne out by the numbers of schools of this type which have achieved excellent academic ratings from educators. The chief argument for men's and women's schools is that there is little opportunity during the week for social activities and more time for concentration on studies. Proponents of this type of education point out that there is invariably a school for the opposite sex nearby.

In discussing this question with young people and their parents, we stress that the decision is a personal one and should be made in terms of the student's desires and, in some cases, on the basis of his personality.

For the student who succumbs to temptation and frequently overemphasizes social activities, it might sometimes be expedient to attend a men's or women's school. However, this in itself is no guarantee that the seeker of pleasures will not be able to find some outlet or means of gratifying his or her desire to mingle with the opposite sex.

One or two previous studies which compared young people of equal ability in both coed and women's colleges have supplied evidence that the girls in the coed situation did as well or better academically than their sisters in the women's colleges.

In recent years, the entire issue has become a moot one, since many of the unisex colleges have converted to coed status. A few colleges permitted their students to vote on this issue and, interestingly enough, many preferred their unisex identity. Some of the female college students had very strong feelings about the greater opportunities for self-expression, development, and administrative experience in a unisex collegiate setting.

COMMUTING vs. LIVING AWAY FROM HOME

This problem is almost always taken care of by your financial situation; however, there are times when the issue is debatable. If there is any possibility of living on campus, the student should make every effort to do so. He may have to convince his parents of the wisdom of this choice, but he should be able to secure assistance from his counselors, who generally are in favor of this type of experience. A number of educators have constantly urged parents to send their children away from home for an education in every sense of the word. They contend that boys and girls living at home are rarely allowed to make their own decisions or to assume real responsibility. They also express strong feelings about the need for students to develop complete independence, a state that is rarely achieved at home. An added reason for considering a school away from home is that most people have a visualization of a college education away from their home environs, and whatever conceptions they may have about it will either be dispelled or strengthened by the actual experience.

A number of students come back after the first year at school to attend local colleges. The year on campus seems to satisfy an adolescent urge to get away; and upon their return, these young people often settle down to the new situation better prepared to accept the fact that education, even if achieved by daily bus, train, or car travel, is still a real education.

Some students choose to delay moving away from home until they have completed their undergraduate degrees. If there are prospects of postgraduate training in a professional school located some distance from home, some thought might be given to delaying the experience of campus residence until that time.

DISTANCE AND TRANSPORTATION PROBLEMS

After finishing her first year at a distant college, one student came back to our school to secure information about college transfer. Although completely happy at the college of her choice, she had found the transportation situation both costly and time consuming. Joan had failed to consider some of the less obvious factors of transportation. Her original visit was made by car, and she did not run through the routine of reaching school by the usual channels. In traveling back and forth on holidays, she learned that she had to take a cab to a bus station, take a bus to the railroad, take either the bus or another train to her home area, and follow it up by bus or taxicab. Unfortunately, the trains ran infrequently, bus service was inadequate, and her plans had to be made relative to the train and bus schedules, Plane trips were of no great help, since she had to take a bus to the airport, then add a lengthy trip once she arrived at the airport nearest home.

To some, this may not be troublesome, but to others it might be well to plan and plot transportation routes to college. Car travel in groups may relieve you of some of the problems that have been mentioned, but then you must have some assurance of the presence on campus of students from your home town.

LARGE vs. SMALL COLLEGE

Size is a major factor in deciding on a school, and this subject merits a great deal of attention. Figures appearing in college guides may give erroneous impressions, as even institutions listing populations of 40,000 may have within their borders a small college with a total population of 1,000. In this sense, the college within the university may be much smaller than an independent small college.

When students discuss college size with us, we tell them that the decision is one that has to be made on an individual basis and that there are several items to keep in mind in attempting to arrive at a decision. From the personality angle, it might seem that the quiet, shy, unaggressive person may make a better adjustment in a smaller school. Opportunities for participation in activities become greater when there are more openings with limited competition. Social adjustment may be easier, since a smaller school enables students to meet each other much more frequently and develop many more intimate acquaintanceships without prearranged planning. Smaller colleges have social activities which bring together the greatest part of the student population and help to generate a comfortable feeling in a short period of time.

In smaller schools, opportunities for meeting instructors and professors seem to be greater. This also promotes a feeling of being wanted and being recognized as an individual rather than as a cog in a very large wheel.

Yet there are disadvantages to the smaller college. It may have fewer course offerings and limited faculty, leaving you with the possibility of having the same professor for several courses. In a small school, the student who has any major personality quirks becomes conspicuous, and any attempt to cover up becomes almost an impossible task in this kind of tightly knit group. Some admissions officers pointedly suggest that the student with unusual characteristics is far better off in a larger school where he may not stand out so obviously. Certainly, anonymity is more easily achieved in a larger institution.

The larger schools have the advantage of offering more courses in different areas, more specialty programs, and frequently, larger libraries and better research facilities. Some young people enjoy the give-and-take of a large institution, relish the competition, and feel pleasantly at home in one of these larger communities. For these young people the decision is not too difficult to make.

Some universities offer liberal arts programs, business administration, engineering, fine arts, medicine, dentistry, etc. Others do not have all of these offerings, but by definition you should recognize that a *university* is an institution of higher learning with several professional schools and faculties, including schools of graduate studies.

A *college* is an institution of higher learning affording a general or liberal rather than technical or professional training. A college may be a unit of a university and, as such, would furnish courses of instruction in a specific field leading to a bachelor's degree.

For those students who are undecided about their careers, attending a university sometimes offers a partial solution to their problems. They may find it easier to transfer within the university from one program to another without loss of too many credits and without having to adjust to an entirely new school environment.

There has been a widespread belief that for those who intend to continue their studies on a graduate level, opportunities for admission to the specific graduate schools of a university are more favorable to those already in attendance at one of the university's colleges. This is not necessarily true. Several years ago we made a study of medical schools and the colleges from which their students came. Using the information found in a number of the medical college catalogs, students conducting the study made tabulations for the different feeding schools. They discovered that medical schools accepted students from many colleges and

Below and **right** *While large universities often offer extensive cultural, research, and teaching resources, smaller colleges and universities offer the benefits of increased individual attention and a more supportive environment.*

OAKLAND UNIVERSITY

that there were many schools outside the university itself that sent more of their graduates than the college which was part of the university.

Some admissions officers state that, all things being equal, students at their college may have a slight advantage over applicants from outside their university in gaining admission to graduate school. However, these admissions people are quick to tell students that expectation of admission to one of their graduate schools is not in itself a good and substantial reason for selecting their university.

Universities do have, on a collective basis, much more prestige than colleges, although individual colleges may be far more renowned than individual universities. Universities do offer opportunities for taking courses in different colleges of the university, and they have the advantage of heavy endowments which enable them to expand their programs. They also secure far more money for research from foundations and the government.

There has been some criticism of the large universities because of the trend to use instructors or graduate assistants on the freshman and sophomore levels, conserving more illustrious professors for upper level classes or for graduate work. Some object to the large lecture classes of some of the universities which may enroll from 100 to 500 students for one weekly lecture and then break them down into discussion groups of 25 for two other sessions during the week under leadership of a graduate fellowship student or a young instructor. This argument may be turned around with ease by the contention of the university that the lecture may be one emanating from a national authority or member of the staff who has written extensively in his field. Colleges operating by themselves, with few exceptions, offer more experienced teachers during the early years of college; contact between instructor and student is a much more frequent and normal type of experience. At the larger universities with strong graduate programs, professors often have definite personal priorities. Often their first interest is their research projects; second in their graduate students; and last and least, the undergraduates.

One approach to making the decision about school size is to visit at least one, if not two, fairly large colleges and universities and balance this with visits to smaller campuses. Look about you, visit classrooms, student lounges, dining rooms, dorms, and athletic facilities, and then stop students to ask a few pertinent questions—"What do you like best about a college of this size?" "What do you like least about your institution?"

The temptation of those of us who are older is to highly endorse the small school, with its real or imagined advantages. But years of experience have taught me to have faith in the judgment of young people. The quiet, timorous young lady applies to a large school, and despite our hesitancy about her selection, we discover that she is persistent. Better still, she makes an excellent adjustment at a school with a population of almost 40,000.

PUBLIC, PRIVATE, OR DENOMINATIONAL SCHOOLS

Before discussing this issue, it might be wise briefly to define each type. A *public college* is one that is supported by public funds, either by a city, county, or state. It offers certain privileges to the residents of the community involved and tends to be preponderantly partial to local people. Tuition rates at public colleges are far more reasonable, since the expenses and costs are underwritten by the communities or political bodies supporting them.

Private colleges are those which have neither religious nor political affiliations. They are primarily nonprofit, and in theory, they open their doors to all people who meet their entrance requirements. Tuition rates at most private schools are far higher; this is a natural consequence of their being underwritten by private endowment, gifts from alumni, and tuition payments. They are an extremely important part of our educational system, since they are not necessarily subject to the whims of politicians or the pressures that come from political bodies. Their part in expanding our educational program and research has been extremely important, and their freedom from undesirable obligations has, in the minds of some educators, added to their importance in our educational setup.

Denominational schools are those colleges affiliated with different religious groups, supported primarily by church funds. They are a very interesting part of our higher educational system. Their tuition rates are moderate, when compared to the private schools, because of the type of support they receive. For the person who is a member of a particular sect or religious group, denominational colleges offer both a college education and an opportunity to be in a setting which has spiritual significance for him. Also, scholarship seekers who are members of the particular group sponsoring a college may have excellent opportunities for special awards.

In considering this type of school, students who are not members of the faith supporting the college should be aware of the religious emphasis and specific requirements in terms of religious courses and chapel attendance. Many denominational schools make special arrangements for those who are not members of their own faith and offer religious courses on a nonsectarian basis.

In our years of experience with colleges, we have found most denominational schools eager and willing to accept applicants of other faiths. The repeated experiences of such students have demonstrated a very fair and considerate type of treatment, and there has been no hesitation on their part to recommend a denominational school for their friends and relatives.

One problem facing a student who is thinking of attending a denominational school is the question of the extent of the religious emphasis and the specific religious demands and requirements that might be made of him. Students considering such schools should analyze their feelings and try to secure a detailed picture of the reactions of others who have been in attendance there.

In evaluating a denominational school, you should check the percentage of members of the related faith who are in attendance. A school with over 90 percent of one faith is, for all practical purposes, announcing its preference for members of its own religious background. There are some exceptions, and there is no reason why you could not ask a direct question about the feelings of the particular college about admitting members of a different faith. Years ago I was given some very honest and direct responses, suggesting that some of my students would be uncomfortable because everything was geared to the specific religion. However, with attendance down, it is possible that a college may not respond with absolute honesty to such an inquiry.

If you are able to secure definitive statistics about the denominational population and discover that over 80 to 90 percent are affiliated with one church, then you should, if you are not a member of that faith, seriously consider another school. Keep in mind that many of the formerly church affiliated schools have shifted their identity to that of a non-sectarian college, with minor church relationships. All of these schools extend invitations to individuals of any faith, race, or ethnic background.

Public colleges, since they are supported by public funds, have an advantage over most private schools. They are able to attract more experienced and better professors because of their higher salary schedules. They also may have larger libraries and better facilities for extensive research. In some of the larger state universities which must accept all students who offer a high school diploma, there is a problem of weeding out students in the freshman year. This lack of selectivity must lead to some confusion until the college instructors have secured enough evidence that some students have been misplaced.

Students should weigh the advantages of a large school—lower tuition rates, the possibility of better instructors, more and better equipment and volumes in the library—against the possible disadvantages—large student bodies, a greater preponderance of students from one locale, and less individual attention.

With the private colleges there is the argument that they have produced more scholars on a ratio basis than the other schools and may offer more intellectual freedom because of their independence.

With all that has been said, there are exceptions in each category. There are some denominational schools which will almost completely limit their population to those of their own faith; there are some public institutions which pay poorly and have inadequately prepared staffs; and there are some private colleges which have practically no standards and contribute very little to the cultural enrichment of our society.

COURSE OFFERINGS

Although previously mentioned, it might be well to review the need for students to check the offerings of different departments within a college, as well as the number of instructors in the subject field. For example, if you propose to major in physics, you should list the offerings in the subject area and then compare one college with another. This may be done in other areas, too, and may prove helpful when there is indecision between one or two colleges. Students who are undecided about their careers should list the courses in a number of areas in which they have indicated some interest.

We can recall one young lady who went to one of the better midwestern schools planning to major in English. Upon her return to discuss a transfer to another college, she mentioned that the major reason for her decision was the limited number of course offerings in English and the lack of depth in the department.

ACCREDITATION—TYPES, MEANING, IMPORTANCE

If at all possible, you should attend an accredited college. This may not prove an iron-clad guarantee of a good education, but in a majority of cases you will derive many benefits.

The basic type of accreditation is that of the regional associations. In the New England area, the New England Association is the regional accrediting body. In the middle states area it is the Middle States Association; in the northwestern part of the United States it is the Northwestern Association, etc.

Attendance at any member college accredited by a regional association makes it much simpler to transfer credits, since these accrediting bodies use the same criteria for evaluation and accreditation. New colleges take a period of time before they may be accredited, but it is still possible to transfer from one of the unaccredited schools if you have maintained a satisfactory record and the receiving college is willing to consider your credits.

Next, if you are preparing for a specific career, it is important to check carefully for accreditation by the many professional accrediting bodies. Accreditation, for example, by the National Architectural Accrediting Board in the field of architecture, by the American Chemical Society in the field of chemistry, by the American Bar Association in the field of law, implies that these colleges have met certain standards set up by the National Boards and should assure you of good, solid professional training. Again, you may still receive professional training in an unaccredited program, but you may not receive the recognition accorded the graduate of an accredited professional program.

We do know of engineering schools which are not accredited but which have successfully placed graduates in engineering positions. We also know of schools whose chemistry programs are not endorsed by the American Chemical Society but are still able to place their graduates as chemists. However, if there were no longer shortages in these two areas, there is every likelihood that employment offers for the graduates of the accredited schools would be far better. We are also certain that employers, in the main, will pay higher salaries and give first consideration to those students who have had the advantage of training in an accredited program.

A word of warning to young people who eventually plan to take state examinations for licensing in a professional field. Check with your State Board of Examiners to secure from them the list of those schools *whose graduates are acceptable and will be allowed to take the state licensing examination.*

SOCIAL LEVELS OF COLLEGE POPULATION

Students go to college in order to secure an education, but many properly look forward to meeting people, socializing, and building up friendships for a lifetime. To increase your chances of making your college adjustment a pleasant one, you should pay some attention to the kind of people who attend, although this sometimes cannot be done too easily. In some cases there are no problems, since many schools go out of their way to include in their student body members of all races, religions, and different economic levels.

There are schools, however, which cater to students from privileged socio-economic levels. This may present problems for you. There is no known way of getting a detached evaluation of schools in this respect, outside of contacting graduates or those in attendance who may be able to enlighten you on this subject. If you resort to this technique, be certain to get a consensus based on the opinions of many rather than a few.

The problem of socialization is not as great as it was a few years ago, since the number of schools with predominantly wealthy student populations is rapidly dwindling. In some instances parents and students have mistakenly attributed "posh" characteristics to schools because of a tendency of many people to stereotype certain institutions. In reality, many of these colleges have from 20 to 33 1/3 percent of their students on scholarship, an indication that at least this percentage of the student body comes from homes with moderate incomes. However, we know that some of these students have been made unhappy by being left out of parties, being snubbed by social clubs, and being members of isolated minorities with restricted activities.

ACADEMIC LEVELS

The question of the academic level of a college is particularly important in evaluating your chances of remaining in good standing at a school. Academic levels of colleges vary considerably. Some contain a population consisting almost entirely of gifted, talented, or very bright students; others have on campus a range of average-to-gifted; still others have students with ability that is concentrated on the above-average level. Statistically speaking, the probabilities of securing an education without being placed on probation or flunking out are much better in a college where your potential and previous academic record place you in a competitive position with your classmates. There are more disadvantages to being "low man on the totem pole" than there are to being average or above average in comparison to your fellow students. Managing to squeeze into a school through political or alumni influence, or gaining late admission after colleges have exhausted their lists, generally signifies that the college accepting you on either of these bases has been able previously to select better-qualified students. Persons with poor records and less academic potential than their classmates will find it difficult to maintain passing grades in such situations.

When standards at practically all colleges were elevated in past years, the assumption that the bottom group should prove to be fair candidates for a degree was not validated by the facts. Now that admission standards have dropped at more than 90 percent of the colleges (at one national meeting that I attended, I heard a comment that at least 50 percent of the colleges had open admissions) and the problem of retention is so great, there has been an altered attitude toward the marginal students. Remediation (assistance with reading, basic math, and study skills), more pass-fail grades for the first year, limited schedules with reduced hours to remove some of the academic pressures, pre-school summer programs to ready students for their new intellectual experiences, and the omission of all failures during the freshman year, with substitution of no-credit grades, have been introduced.

There is no question that the aforementioned procedures have assisted marginal students in their collegiate adjustment. Notwithstanding all of this, in order to ensure success, you would be well

advised to choose a school where you will be close to the middle of the group in academic ability.

URBAN, SEMI-URBAN, OR RURAL SETTING

The country youth may sometimes find it difficult to adjust to a city setting, and the city-bred student may become disenchanted with a completely rural setting. This issue has come up in discussions with students who have been away at college, and obviously, it should be given some consideration in the process of selecting a school. The question must be answered on an individual basis, and a week-end stay on campus may help considerably.

Proximity to large cities with their cultural advantages may be important to some students. Some colleges in rural settings take care of this problem by bringing in many guest speakers and artists to entertain their student population. If you are conditioned to going down to the corner drugstore and having theaters and other facilities close at hand, and if your tolerance for the sound of crickets is not too great, you may well consider location in an urban or at least a semi-urban setting.

There is much to be said for the school located in the city, with or without the lovely green campus. These schools may rightfully advertise that the city, with its tremendous advantages, is the actual campus, offering an education in itself with its concerts, lectures, dramatic presentations, movie houses, restaurants with different national settings, and sections of the city which are inhabited predominantly by members of various racial and ethnic groups.

Some students feel that an education is not a true one unless the lawns are finely manicured and the paths lined with trees. As

Left *Urban, semi-urban, and rural colleges all have unique advantages.*

a result, they sometimes look down upon some of the finest schools because they do not offer such environmental advantages. They later learn that it is possible to secure an education in an institution that does not have a physically attractive setting.

LOCATION

Experience has taught us that one of the factors that has increased in importance in the issue of selecting a college is the actual location of the college and its dormitories. For some students, a college located in a big city may result in restricting evening travel. Again, for students living in off-campus quarters because of overcrowded conditions at the college, a check should be made on the type of area through which they may have to travel daily to and from school. With the changes which have been taking place in many cities, this problem has become accentuated, and from year to year more students have reminded us to forewarn our high school students about this situation.

LIBRARY

Besides looking at the campus, you also would profit by checking the library, the number of books within the library, and the use of the library by students. A check of catalogs and college guides will show colleges having from 10,000 to more than 5,000,000 volumes. The latter is an unusual figure, and you should not expect to find many schools with numbers running over the 100,000 level. If you are interested in doing research and securing a good education, look for the college which has a good library. You may also discover by a visit to the library how much it is used by the students. This sometimes serves as a good measure of the intellectual curiosity of the student body.

RATIO OF STUDENTS TO FACULTY

Many college guides offer some picture of the number of faculty members, then give a teacher to student ratio—one faculty member to eight, or one to as many as 30. These figures are not too meaningful, since some of the faculty members may teach only one or two classes and devote the rest of their time to research. It is also conceivable that administrative officials and counseling personnel are included in this ratio.

However, on the average, the school which lists the lowest ratio *should* provide students with smaller classes. Smaller classes mean more individual attention and greater opportunity for self-expression. I have been in classes at universities with more than 150 sitting in the lecture hall, and I have also had the pleasure of participating in a seminar with only eight. Small classes have innumerable advantages. Your best bet for securing meaningful statistics is by querying different students when visiting the school, or by asking definitive questions of admissions officials.

YEAR-ROUND CAMPUS

Adding to the complications of making a decision about a school is the practice of many more colleges offering school programs on a year-round basis. Many colleges have introduced trimester, four-quarter, year-round programs, or other accelerated schedules to expedite the completion of college in less than the four years. Institutions of all sizes and types have adopted year-round programs—from enrollments of less than 1,000 to university populations over the 15,000 mark.

At one time most schools were organized around a two-semester plan, with the option of summer school attendance. In recent years, a certain amount of confusion with the nomenclature of the new systems that are rapidly coming into use has been created. Whether a school advertises a quarter plan, a trimester plan, or two terms plus summer session plan is not the all-important issue. The problem is deciding whether to attend schools offering one of these programs, with the possibility of completing four years of college in less than three years. Practically all schools with such plans encourage students to attend year-round but do not make this form of attendance compulsory.

The Fund for the Advancement of Education published a pamphlet entitled *The Year-Round Campus Catches On,* which reported that public reaction to such plans is favorable, many students endorse the program, and several states recommend the programs as practical and feasible. Certainly young people who are going into graduate fields could find these programs a means of cutting down on the amount of time they will spend in school. It might be practical for prospective students to investigate some of these programs. Costs are higher, since the work is concentrated, and the student who is dependent on summer earnings may find that participation in this type of program may create financial difficulties.

ATTENDING SCHOOLS OUTSIDE YOUR DISTRICT

If you needed proof of the congested conditions in public colleges, you could receive it by comparing admission policies of state schools ten years ago and today. A great many of the state institutions at one time prided themselves on the fact that their students came from all corners of the United States, considering it extremely important to attract young people from different sections of the country. Recently, however, even the staunchest advocates have had to re-evaluate this policy because of pressures within their own state boundaries to serve resident students.

If you happen to be interested in a state university, you could conserve a great deal of your time by finding out their latest policy for out-of-state residents. We always suggest to our students that they submit a brief resume of their school record, their practice test scores (if required), and the branch of the school or university in which they are interested. All responses are not completely definitive, but they at least give some indication of the opportunities for gaining admission.

Don't allow yourself to be trapped into the notion that a state school, with limited openings for out-of-staters, is necessarily a better or more competitive school. A few institutions with restrictive admissions policies for non-residents have an open admissions policy for their own population.

There are still variations in policy from state to state, so that you do not have to eliminate the possibility of gaining admission to an out-of-state university. However, protect yourself by getting some picture of the present situation. A few of the state universities flatly refuse to send many students application blanks, and some pointedly suggest that application be made to other schools. Some offer figures on the number of out-of-staters they may admit and, occasionally, the number of out-of-state people who have applied.

Keep in mind that policies change from year to year—read the fine lines on admissions policies for out-of-state students. If you think you might qualify for admission, file an application and let the college make the decision. Disregard the rumor part or the word of an acquaintance who picked up his information from a second cousin who once dated a girl whose father attended the school in question.

One good source of information on state university policies is the annual publication *College Admissions Data,* published by the Educational Research Corporation, 85 Main Street, Watertown, Massachusetts 02172. Since this is a costly directory, try to utilize your guidance office copy, or attempt to persuade them to purchase this excellent resource. Issued annually in two volumes, this loose-leaf publication includes solid informational sketches of over 700 institutions. Photocopying pages concerned with different institutions is an effective method of gathering and accumulating information about schools of interest to you.

GEOGRAPHICAL FACTORS

For students, Horace Greeley's maxim, "Go west," has taken on added meaning in the quest for selective college admission. Most colleges are eager to have a geographically representative population on campus, and in their catalogs, they often give a breakdown of their student body by states and by foreign countries. This desire for geographic variety in the student body has resulted in location becoming a factor in college placement. We have found over a period of years that distance lends enchantment and that a student considered marginal by a local college is welcomed by a college at a distance of 500 to 1,000 miles. This does not mean that you will *automatically* gain acceptance by choosing a college 1,000 miles from home, but it does imply a greater likelihood of success.

The delay and frustration of applying to eastern prestige college could easily be remedied if many of the applicants applied to the better midwestern, southern, and far western colleges. A few years ago one of my counselees, after applying to a number of so-called prestige colleges, sent his College Board scores to a well-rated midwestern college, without forwarding an application. The school dropped him a very pleasant note complimenting him on his excellent scores and indicating an interest in him. The institution has a faculty of over 97 percent who have their Ph.D.'s, excellent laboratory and library facilities, a good placement record for graduate schools, and is sufficiently endowed to assist any needy applicant.

As you select a college, give major emphasis to this factor of geographic location. Remember that there are exciting colleges in all areas of our country which are making major academic contributions.

EXPERIMENTAL PROGRAMS AND CURRICULA

During the past few years, many students have expressed interest in experimental curricula. They apparently are seeking college programs which are new and different, and counselors should keep such curricula in mind as they assist in the selection of a college. There is not a single comprehensive directory listing innovative or experimental curricula, but there are several individual publications which discuss them, including: *Meet the Challenge,* published by the B'Nai B'rith Career and Counseling Services, Washington, D.C.; *Directory of Free Universities and Experimental Colleges,* Center for Educational Reform, Washington, D.C.; and *Models and Mavericks: A Profile of Private Liberal Arts Colleges,* published by McGraw-Hill Books in 1971.

Many schools have widely varied programs, and it would be wise not to rely solely on some of the well-publicized experimental schools. Innovative programs that might be considered are offered by: Antioch, Bard, Beloit, Blackburn, Colorado College, Evergreen State, Franconia, Friends World, Goddard, Hampshire, Hiram, Livingston (Rutgers), Manhattanville, New, Oakland University, Simon's Rock, St. John's (Maryland and New Mexico), and Webster. Further research will reveal many more schools with non-traditional curricula.

CHAPTER 4

THE RATING OF COLLEGES

Students frequently ask counselors how one school compares to another. They are curious about statements that such-and-such a college has a much higher rating than other schools. There is no rating system for colleges that is universally accepted, but some counselors rate colleges on the following criteria:

- Their admission requirements.
- The picture of the school given by many of its students over a period of time.
- The success of these students in gaining admission to so-called better schools of graduate study.
- Students' college grades as compared to the grades received in high school.
- The quality of the faculty.
- Adequacy of the library and other facilities.

This method is obviously very subjective. We know that entrance requirements vary according to geographic distribution and religious, racial, and national background. A school may set stringent admission standards for local applicants and quite conceivably consider students with lower marks and less potential if they reside 1,000 miles away from the college.

Variations in admissions requirements often are based on special standards for different college programs or for individual schools within universities. By way of illustration, a selective college offering a program in agriculture may consider the admission of agriculture candidates quite differently than liberal arts applicants, and a number of schools are more liberal in their standards for engineering students than for some other majors.

OTHER RATING SYSTEMS

A few years ago there was a flood of information about the so-called best colleges in a number of areas. These ratings were based on the number of students of the college who went on to graduate studies and on the number of graduates who achieved renown by being listed in *Who's Who* in the science field or other areas.

This approach did not supply a valid system of rating colleges; however, it did submit names of little-known schools, making it conceivable that in the future, these schools may become very well known to more people.

If you are interested in some of the schools that have been listed, you may secure information by checking Robert H. Knapp's and Hubert E. Goodrich's *Origins of American Scientists,* and Robert H. Knapp's and Joseph J. Greenbaum's *The Younger American Scholar: His Collegiate Origins,* both published by the University of Chicago Press. Although dated, these sources can be most helpful and may reveal some schools that might normally be overlooked.

To illustrate how difficult it is to develop an accurate appraisal of "good" colleges, a study by Alexander Astin, formerly a member of the National Merit Scholarship Corporation, disclosed that the selective New England men's colleges were significantly deficient in the number of graduate scholars they produced when compared to less prestigious schools.

Such directories as Cass & Birnbaum's and Barron's, which offer rating lists of colleges that are *most selective, highly selective, very selective,* and *selective,* indicate that these evalua- tive terms are not ratings at all, but are intended merely to offer guidance. Although there are definitive explanations of the rating terms and guarded suggestions for their use, many students and their parents constantly quote them as if they were official. A typical question is, "How can you recommend _____ college when it is only rated *selective* and not offer _____ college which is rated *most selective*?" Again, the directory editors have most likely based their ratings on the caliber of the student population, background of faculty, and the adequacy of facilities. Certainly a measuring tool has not been developed that would be sufficiently comprehensive and reliable enough to please exacting statisticians.

In 1965, Alexander Astin assembled comprehensive statistical information about selected colleges' students, atmosphere, and curricula. He published his findings in Science Research Associates' *Who Goes Where To College,* which supplied readers with the most meaningful rating of colleges to date. If Astin's information were brought up to date and expanded to include all colleges, we would have, in my estimation, the best picture of the relative ratings of colleges.

PRESTIGE COLLEGES

Much of the confusion and delay in college admissions is caused by the great number of students who hope to be admitted to the so-called *select* colleges—the Ivy League and prestige women's colleges (some of which are now merged or closely related); some of the smaller but well-known private colleges in the East; and a few schools in the Midwest and on the Pacific coast. Increased persistence for admission to these schools frequently has been based on the notion that graduation from one of them will guarantee prestige, excellent graduate or professional school placement, status, proper contacts for business purposes, and open doors to select social circles.

There is no question that these schools have been able to attract some of the most capable students in the country. But their small size has created problems of admission and has also led to greater selectivity on their part.

Is this fight for admission worth the effort? Some of the admissions directors of these prestige schools, as pleased as they are with the number of applicants, believe that too many students delude themselves in thinking that only these institutions can offer a good education. These admissions officers are fully aware of the excellent academic status of other institutions and recognize that many of these schools have produced illustrious graduates.

Admittedly, students who attend prestige schools enjoy many advantages. However, applicants should also consider the disadvantages which may be associated with such institutions.

The possibility of social rejection at one of these schools is great, which can result in severe mental anguish. Because their costs are quite high, such schools tend to attract students from high economic levels. Although these schools also entertain many scholarship students, there may be a great danger of a feeling of "not belonging" in this type of setting. With the ability of the prestige school to attract many capable students, you may be faced with more academic competition than you encountered in your high school. Added to this is the problem of competing with graduates of private schools who have had tutoring and other scholastic advantages which momentarily place them ahead of the public high school graduate. It should be pointed out, however, that several studies have demonstrated that, in the long run, the public school graduate of equal ability will eventually surpass the private school graduate in academic achievement.

Part of the anxiety over admission to prestige colleges is based on the excellent records these schools have established in placing their graduates in schools of medicine, law, etc. This excellent track record is based on the fact that, instead of waiting to screen

their students in college, they subject all their applicants to a very careful admissions process which automatically eliminates poor candidates for graduate studies. Successful graduate school placement, therefore, frequently is based on this screening factor; the same students, if placed in any other accredited college or university, would most likely meet with the same success.

PRESTIGE COLLEGES OF THE FUTURE

In addition to the selected few colleges and universities which have traditionally been considered prestige institutions, there are many *other* schools which have already achieved prestige status in the eyes of many educators and students. It is likely that many more will be added to the list in the near future, but at the present time it includes such schools as: Reed, Rice, Oberlin,

Carleton, Grinnell, Wabash, Earlham, Knox, Vanderbilt, New, the Claremont Colleges, Colorado, and Lawrence. A few years ago students had to be urged to consider many of these colleges which now are recognized among the most desirable and competitive schools in the country.

The point is a simple one. There are many good schools, large and small, which may not be well-known at the present time, but which have already produced excellent scholars and have received nationwide status and recognition. If you are looking for a good education, ask your counselor about the names of some of these excellent schools which may not be well-known in your own area. If you want to prove your resourcefulness, you might check *Origins of American Scientsts* and *The Younger American Scholar: His Collegiate Origins* for colleges which have produced

Left and below *Careful consideration should be given to the course offerings available at the college you choose.*

HUXLEY COLLEGE

scholars and scientists and prepare a list of schools from these sources.

WHAT IS THE BEST COLLEGE?

Instead of thinking purely in terms of prestige, you should select a college which best suits your abilities and needs. Why attempt to place yourself in water over your head by attending a school where the majority of the student body is far ahead of you academically? Why consider a school where you may feel uncomfortable economically and socially? Psychological factors should not be overlooked. Your self-image and self-concept are of utmost importance in academic, emotional, and social growth.

There are definitely some colleges in which you can feel comfortable socially, academically, and financially. Admission to one of these schools should lead to a pleasant four years, the possibility of a good education within your own limits, and the pleasure of making acquaintances who are willing to accept you.

CHAPTER 5

SPECIALIZED OR LIBERAL ARTS EDUCATION?

In our earlier definition of university and college, we briefly mentioned *specialized colleges.* These are institutions which have very specialized programs in particular occupational areas, i.e., engineering schools, teachers colleges, music and fine arts schools, medical schools, and business administration. In making a decision about higher education, you may have to decide between attendance at a liberal arts college or one of these specialized schools.

This issue often has been debated without any final resolution. Those who argue for the liberal arts education stress the following: most people change their occupational plans many times, and it is relatively easy to effect change within the broad background of a liberal arts program; many employers have learned to respect the broad liberal arts education and will hire and then train such graduates; still others believe that since a liberal arts education is generally exacting and demanding, the graduate of this program secures immediate recognition in almost all pursuits. Some of the colleges have put out brochures expanding on these arguments and offering other advantages of a liberal arts education.

Opponents of liberal arts programs believe that they devote too much course work to nonessentials. Expanding this argument, they state that in our present era of specialization, the need is for greater emphasis in particular fields. In addition, they point to the present trend within many specialized schools of adding a

broad liberal arts base to their educational programs. In these curricula, required subjects include many of the same ones taken in a liberal arts program for the first two years, after which emphasis is placed on the major subject or field of specialization.

Conversely, many liberal arts colleges are stressing the specialized training available within their programs. They point out that you can major in biology, microbiology, chemistry, political science, or physics, and upon graduation, secure employment in one of these specialized fields.

As a general rule, we recommend the liberal arts program to most students. This recommendation is based on the assumption that liberal arts colleges tend to be more stringent in their scholastic requirements. In the past they have been able, with the possible exception of engineering colleges and technological institutes, to attract the more capable students. Academic standards have been maintained, and the result has been graduates who have excelled in many areas.

In the case of universities with their many divisions, we have learned over a period of years that, generally, admission standards vary considerably for applicants to the different colleges. Although many universities do not publish the differences, counselors have learned to a certain extent how to adapt the type of applicants to the different colleges of the university. For example, one of the larger eastern universities rejected an applicant ranked in the top one-fourth of his class for its premedical program and accepted a mid-ranked student for its school of business administration. Such incidents have led counselors to recognize the possible academic effects of greater competition in liberal arts programs.

We would suggest that if you are looking for a challenging, broad education, your opportunities for securing this background

Left *The choice of specializing or earning a more general liberal arts degree is a key factor in deciding which college is best for you.*

probably would be much greater in a liberal arts program than in a specialized curriculum. You may supplement this program with either graduate studies in a particular field or with specialized courses taken during summer sessions.

On the other hand, if you are pressed for time and expect to specialize, your best choice would be direct application to a specialized school. If you are hesitant about a career choice and are eager for intellectual competition, your opportunities for achieving this will be greater in the liberal arts program.

ENGINEERING

If the word has not seeped down to you, you should be alerted to the fact that many who enter the engineering field or an engineering school do not complete their education in their chosen field. Perhaps we may be overly aware of this because of the number of our students who have shifted from engineering programs to other fields. Distorted notions about the curriculum and the mistaken concept that skill with an erector set or in the use of tools foreshadows success in the engineering field offer a partial explanation of the shift out of such programs. Exacting standards that do not permit errors add to the removal of students from such programs. Additionally, some switch because they lament the lack of intellectual stimulation and the apolitical or conservative nature of many engineering students. Some engineering college officials have admitted that these factors have created a major problem for which they cannot offer any complete solution. They point out, however, that there is a comparable amount of shifting within liberal arts fields of specialization and in other special programs.

One possible solution to this problem of program switching is the three-two and two-three plan, which permits engineering candidates to secure two or three years of liberal arts training and then complete their education with two or three years in an engineering school. Upon graduation, they are qualified to hold employment as engineers. The advantage of participating in this type of program is that with maturity and the additional liberal arts background, you may be far more certain of your desire and readiness to enter the engineering field. This readiness must be stressed, since many young people have selected the engineering field because of a childhood fantasy or as part of a distorted picture of what engineers actually do. Such illusions generally are shattered in the first year of engineering school when students are faced with the requirements and demands of a rigorous, specialized program.

Some engineering schools have broadened their liberal arts program in the first year and believe that students are protected by this new approach. If the student discovers that he is really not interested in engineering, he may transfer to another major field or any other type of college without a great loss of credits or time.

For those who are considering engineering as a career (and there are many job opportunities and a great need for trained people in this field), the following steps are suggested:

• Read as much as you can about the requirements for the field, using good occupational pamphlets and brochures.

• Get the names of several engineers in different fields, contact and query them in order to secure a better picture of what is involved.

• Check the possible types of training for the field of engineering, and, if undecided, give serious consideration to the three-two or two-three plan.

• If time is of the essence, making you feel that you cannot afford the extra year for liberal arts study, review the catalogs of engineering colleges and ensure the possibility of a simple transfer without too much loss of credit by selecting those schools which place less emphasis on specialized training in the first year.

LAW SCHOOLS

In these hectic days of competitive admissions and heavy emphasis on grades, most law schools in the United States specify a baccalaureate degree, not specific courses, as a requirement for admission. Additionally, they make widespread use of the Law School Admission Test (LSAT).

It is possible to predict approximate LSAT performance by increasing and decreasing a student's higher verbal score on the Scholastic Aptitude Test by thirty points and using these two figures as the expected scoring range. This crude method of prediction is mentioned here for the benefit of aspiring lawyers with low verbal SAT scores. By participating in an intensive reading program throughout their four years of college, such students can improve their vocabularies and reading comprehension, thus increasing the likelihood of their doing well on the LSAT's.

Since the law schools do not make excessive demands in specific subject areas, a number of our students have been able to combine another occupation with their law training. Some have attended schools of business administration, frequently specializing in accounting, then have attended a law school. Thus they have been trained as both accountants and lawyers. Others have trained as engineers, then moved on to law school. One could, for instance, first train as a history teacher, scientist, economist, psychologist, or chemist, and then secure law school training. Majoring in another subject while preparing to enter the law field has many advantages and might lead to a specialization that could prove highly remunerative.

MEDICAL SCHOOLS

As more and more young people have become interested in health careers, applications to medical schools have been multiplying. As they increase, the Grade Point Averages (GPA's) and test scores continue to become more and more competitive. Some medical schools have over 8,000 applications for 120 openings. These figures may be misleading because of multiple applications, but we do know that of three qualified medical school applicants, only one will secure a place in an American school. All of this sets up the ripple effect, with shifting of some applicants to dental schools. As the dental schools become more selective, there is a spillover to such other health-allied fields as chiropody and optometry, making these schools more competitive. Some students decide to go the foreign medical school route, begetting a spate of enterprising agencies that will assist you (for sums from $1,000 to $4,000) in securing admission to a foreign institution and in language training.

To avoid these exhorbitant charges, which are *not* necessary, seek out approved counseling services or contact your local American Medical Association Society. If you happen to be conveniently located, consider requesting assistance from the Admissions Directors of nearby medical schools. Any one of these sources could assist you in formulating meaningful plans for placement in a foreign medical school. A recent publication, *Medical Careers Planning Book,* by Drs. Attia Naseem and Kamil Mustafa (Bureau of Health and Hospital Career Counseling, P.O. Box 238, Scarsdale, New York 10583), has excellent information about placement in foreign medical schools. Since the volume is rather expensive, you might try to borrow a copy from your local library. Another good information source is the *Guide to Foreign Medical Schools,* by Dr. D. Marien (Press Institute of International Education, 809 United National Plaza, New York, N.Y. 10017).

ADMISSION TO PROFESSIONAL SCHOOLS

This chapter began with a discussion on the question of liberal arts program vs. specialized schools and has veered into the question of securing professional training (engineering, law, and medicine). Perhaps it might now be advantageous to raise the entire issue of admission to professional schools. With many college students in preprofessional training, the problem of moving on to the next educational level should be given some consideration at the same time undergraduate college selection is taking place. In another section we commented on the possible advantages of attendance at a prestige school for gaining admission to a medical school. The thoughts expressed are still applicable—namely, that any college with an accredited preprofessional program can assist a good scholar in entering his chosen field, subject to the existing competition, available openings, and specific aptitude test score.

Students who aspire to professional schools of optometry, chiropody, dentistry, veterinary medicine, and pharmacy should make certain that their intended colleges offer the courses which meet the requirements or have the preprofessional accreditation demanded by professional schools. Such students might also do well to check catalogs of a number of professional schools to be certain that minimum course requirements are being provided in preprofessional training. It would also prove profitable to check state board requirements and get a list of approved professional schools.

Without being too defeatist, every student should give some thought to second or third occupational choices, since there is, to say the least, heightened competition for admission to all professional schools.

COOPERATIVE (WORK-STUDY) SCHOOLS

The cooperative plan of education traditionally has called for five years of combined school and work. Recently, however, some junior colleges have allowed students to combine work experience and studies to earn an associate of arts degree within two years, and more and more four-year colleges are programming work-study within a four-year schedule. Such programs vary from college to college but essentially are based on three to six months' attendance in college and a corresponding period on the job. Placement on the job may be close to the college or in the vicinity of your own home. Colleges will aid you in job placement but prefer, if possible, that you handle this yourself.

There has been a vast extension of the number of schools participating in this program. Its practical nature appeals to many students and offers the following advantages: studies may be related directly to work-theory; for those who are undecided about a career, this plan enables them to test their adaptability to a particular kind of work in the field; and if affords them an opportunity to pay wholly or in part for their education after the first year.

There also are some disadvantages to be considered in work-study plans. A planned social life becomes difficult in this situation, since students are coming and going at different intervals. Additionally, picking up study after working for several months may prove to be troublesome, and the months spent in inconsequential jobs may prove boring and tedious.

If you are interested in cooperative education, you should secure a list of such programs from the various directories and colleges guides available in your guidance counselor's office. You also can write to the National Commission for Cooperative Education, 360 Huntington Avenue, Boston, Massachusetts 02115, for the most current list of schools. Read the catalogs carefully to evaluate the work-study programs. Again, we would urge you to try to contact some students who have attended colleges offering the cooperative plan of education to secure their reactions. Remember that it is much more meaningful to talk to as many students as possible to minimize the element of distortion which might result from only one or two contacts.

CHAPTER 6

GETTING INTO COLLEGE

The criteria used by colleges in the selection of students vary, but the following (*not* listed in order of importance) are the major factors admissions committees consider:

- Rank in high school class
- Recommendations from principal, counselor, and teachers
- Special entrance test scores—aptitude, achievement, etc.
- Participation in extracurricular activities
- Prizes or distinctions won in any field
- Personality ratings
- Personal interviews
- College background of parents
- Letters of reference
- Student's autobiography
- Religious background
- Recommendation from an alumni group
- Work and/or volunteer experiences

THE MOST IMPORTANT FACTORS

At the end of a school year counselors sometimes wonder whether they can really decide what is most important. For example, a very select school turned down a senior who had close to an "A" average and whose SAT scores were over 600, with Achievement Test scores in the same vicinity. This very same school accepted a student who had a "B" average, slightly lower SAT scores, and fewer extracurricular activities. This story, with some variations, is repeated often enough to make the job of counseling students on college admissions an extremely difficult one.

In the main, emphasis for admission is on class rank, test results, and the principal's or counselor's recommendation. Of course, our face was very red recently when a college turned down a student whom we have recommended highly and accepted one of our seniors who had received only a lukewarm endorsement.

A partial explanation of why some students are chosen over others may be personality factors or the impression they make during interviews. In other cases, the reasons for selection may be traced to attitudes of interviewers or reactions of admissions committees to a small, isolated statement made by an applicant. Sometimes, if the student is a member of a religious minority group, he must be prepared to recognize that he may have to offer more in terms of grades, test scores, and activities than other applicants. Still other minority applicants who are culturally disadvantaged may offer lower GPA's, minimal test scores, and few activities and still gain admission. The liberalization of acceptance policies for some minority groups is largely compensation for our past failures to offer equal educational opportunities to all individuals, but by and large, exceptions made for minority students are not excessive.

For most colleges, except prestige schools and out-of-state universities, you may use class rank, test scores, and recommendations with some confidence in predicting opportunities for admission. It is necessary to qualify predictions, though, because of the problem of multiple applications and the increase in the number of college-bound students. Counselors may be able to tell you what might have happened a year ago but can only give you an estimate of what your chances would be during your senior year. Most counselors will recommend a "safety" school where admission is almost guaranteed, and it is always wise to give serious consideration to such a suggestion.

VISITING COLLEGES

Almost all schools would like to have you visit them, but this is not mandatory in most cases. There are a few schools where a visit, coupled with an interview, is expected. In addition to the importance colleges attach to campus visits, it is beneficial to you, personally, to familiarize yourself with the colleges in which you are interested before you make a final choice. A large percentage of students never see their college until the first day of school. Any firsthand, advance knowledge about a college should help make your adjustment more pleasant and comfortable. Another reason for visiting is that you or your parents will be investing large sums of money, and you cannot depend on brochures for an accurate description of facilities and accommodations. Visits to colleges also give you some basis for comparison in making your final selection. Campus atmospheres do vary considerably, and you should be able to judge the climate of a school by talking with students and asking them questions about areas of interest to you.

There are several reasons for visiting colleges:

• Psychologically, it is sensible to become familiar with a new setting to reduce the sense of strangeness when you begin classes.

• Seeing your college in action will enable you to gather information about the educational program, the facilities, the *esprit de corps,* and the atmosphere of the school.

• You may gain a better picture of the students with whom you will be associated, observe the kind of community in which the college is located, and view the physical facilities you may be using.

• You will garner firsthand information about the transportation situation and associated costs which you will have to consider.

If colleges mention in their literature preferred dates, seasons, or years (junior or senior) for visits, you should comply with their preferences. In the main, you should decide during your junior year of high school which schools you prefer and should begin your visits toward the end of that year. Try to arrange your visits when the college is in session; this will allow you to sit in on classes and speak to students who may supply you with interesting sidelights on the school. If there is any doubt in your mind about the college calendar, consult the school's catalog to make certain you will arrive when classes are in regular session.

All visits to colleges should be preceded by a note to the admissions office giving the expected date and time of your arrival. You might request an acknowledgment. We suggest that you include a self-addressed postcard, making it possible for them merely to check off their awareness and expectation of your proposed visit. If you definitely expect to apply to this school, be ready to answer questions about your academic record. If you have taken practice College Boards, ACT's, or other tests, have this data with you. *Do not flaunt your test scores.*

INTERVIEWS

Some colleges request personal interviews, and if a catalog indicates that an interview is desirable, it is up to you to make the necessary arrangements. If the college you have selected is at a great distance and you are unable to visit the school, you should write and ask for alternate interview arrangements within your own area. Some colleges make arrangements to have their representatives visit large cities throughout the United States to conduct these interviews.

When colleges indicate that they do not *require* interviews but do *recommend* them, most young people are in a quandary. They are fearful that failure to visit the school may be misinterpreted as a lack of interest on their part and thus may jeopardize their chances for admission. Since we cannot judge the intentions of any staff, a simple rule of thumb would be to schedule interviews for all schools that are of prime interest to you. Schools which are of secondary importance to you but which are within a reasonable driving distance might also be considered.

Prepare yourself for your interview by paying particular attention to your appearance, grooming, and conduct. Most important, read the catalog of the school very carefully. *This is a must,* because you will appear absurd if you ask questions whose answers you should already know. Your knowledge of the school, based on previous reading, will also give some indication of your sincere interest in it.

Most personal interviews are of a very routine nature, with the interviewer being extremely pleasant. Every effort is made to make you feel comfortable, and the purpose is simply to get a picture of you and search for any major, obvious defects. You may be expected to answer the usual stock questions about your interests, plans, school activities, career, hobbies, etc. Give some thought to these possible questions without actually preparing memorized responses. Try to be as natural as possible; avoid affectations and be ready to acknowledge that you do not have answers to some of the questions.

Occasionally you may encounter some interviewers who, considering themselves amateur psychologists, analyze every statement you make. Fortunately such interviewers are rare, but you should be prepared to adapt yourself to any situation. The most disconcerting interviews students can experience are those conducted by very bored interviewers. In some instances of this nature, the college did not solicit the interview, and its overworked staff had to acknowledge students' demands politely.

In other cases, the interviewer may have been speaking with so many prospective candidates that he is unable to keep up the pretense of being interested. Despite the ill feeling this experience creates, you should not allow this disappointment to affect your decision about the school. Remember that the interviewer is just a small cog in the institutional wheel, and it is not likely that you will be taking courses with him. We would recommend that you keep the following in mind during an interview:

- Be as natural as you possibly can.
- Read the school's catalog carefully, then ask only those questions which it does not answer.
- Be prepared to answer questions about your career plans and reasons for selection of the college.
- Be ready to discuss your leisure-time pursuits.
- A question may be posed about your reading habits. If you are unable to supply ample evidence of conversance with the books you mention, your chances of gaining admission could be reduced. Supply your interviewers with titles of books with which you are completely familiar and about which you can maintain an intelligent conversation.
- Be honest—there are some who will argue against this, but honesty will be greatly appreciated. Remember that those who are in the educational field have an appreciation of honesty and look with disfavor on duplicity. If you should be asked why you selected the college, do not give a stilted, artificial response. If it was recommended by your counselor, say so. If you were impressed by the catalog or had heard of it from an alumnus, advance these facts simply and directly. If you are still uncertain about whether you wish to attend this school, admit that you are still in a dilemma. This practice of placing your cards on the table may occasionally boomerang, but in most cases will give a favorable impression.
- Don't offer your test scores, no matter how outstanding, unless the interviewer requests them.

• Don't boast about your accomplishments, academic or otherwise, unless direct questioning is used to bring out this information.

It would pay to heed especially the last two "don'ts," since it is so easy to antagonize an interviewer or any individual by announcing your virtues, achievements, etc. A little humility will go a long way in an interview.

Some of you may come back from college visits with elated reactions based on interviews you thought favorable. Do not allow these experiences to delude you about possible acceptance. A few optimistic chance remarks by a pleasant interviewer are not sufficient cause for undue excitement.

Look forward to your interviews. Every attempt will be made to make you feel comfortable, and rarely will you be asked any embarrassing questions. Most interviewers are skilled technicians in their field and will do everything in their power to bring out the best in you.

Group interviews are becoming quite standard for the purpose of responding to questions raised by prospective applicants. Such sessions are rarely used as a means of rating or evaluating individual students. Many schools also are conducting visitation days with prepared programs. When the students arrive on campus, they often are invited to participate in a group interview.

The National Vocational Guidance Association has published an excellent brochure, *How to Visit Colleges,* which would be good preparation for your visit and interview. The address is 1607 New Hampshire Avenue N.W., Washington, D.C. 20009. The price is $.75. You might ask your counselor for his copy or request him to order some for a group of students.

ROLE OF PARENTS DURING INTERVIEWS

Your parents will probably accompany you on your visits. If you have an appointment with the admissions officer, it is your appointment and *not theirs*. If the admissions officer or representative asks you whether your parents are with you, mention that they are outside. If he invites them into the interview, they should be ready to participate.

We strongly advise you, therefore, to prepare your parents for the possibility of being part of the interview. You should also impress upon them the importance of *not* answering questions for you, even if you have made mistakes and seem to be floundering. If questions are directed to them they should answer directly and briefly. Admissions counselors tend to question a student's maturity and independence when they see parents take over during an interview. Try to stress this with your parents.

ETIQUETTE FOLLOWING A VISIT

Among the pleasant rarities in the lives of counselors are the occasional thank-you notes they receive from students and parents they have helped. We would suggest that you retain a list of people who have spent time with you during your college visit and show them your appreciation by sending them thank-you notes. If any member of the admissions office staff has devoted some time to you, he would appreciate this consideration on your part. There is no need to be gushy or to use flowery language in expressing your thanks.

LETTERS OF REFERENCE

Many colleges request letters of reference or reference sources. There are some people who foolishly believe that college admissions officers will be impressed by letters from mayors, presidents of big corporations, governors, senators, etc. If the letters from these sources are based on personal acquaintance with you and give evidence of knowing about your personality make-up, then they have significance. If, however, they appear to be secondhand references, they are meaningless.

Colleges would prefer simple, descriptive letters from your teachers rather than a politically or commercially inspired reference. We have been through enough conferences with admissions officers to know how highly they regard the words of teachers or persons whose descriptions are based on firsthand knowledge of the student. Actually, you may harm your chances by resorting to a political type of reference, since these letters may offend the intelligence of the admissions committees.

Flooding the admissions office with letters of reference that have not been requested can have an adverse effect. "Bat" Thrasher, retired director of admissions at M.I.T., once said that M.I.T. had a simple rule of thumb about unwanted letters of reference. "The thicker the folder, the thicker the student."

When counselees ask me to send letters of reference, I tell those whom I know only slightly that I have to base the letters on the records rather than on a personal knowledge of their abilities and aptitudes. I strongly urge that they use teachers or faculty advisers who have worked with or taught them and are familiar with their capabilities. My reluctance is based on the knowledge that the strong endorsement given by the teacher or faculty adviser will carry much more weight.

Incidentally, you should *always* secure prior permission from any individual whose name is to be used as a reference. *This is an absolute must.* You should also be sure you have his consent to submit his name as a reference to more than one school.

HIGH SCHOOL RECOMMENDATIONS

This is an important topic, since recommendations from the guidance office or from the principal are requested for all applications. You may wonder on what basis these officials can give you a recommendation. In an ideal situation, they would be acquainted with you and would base their recommendations on this personal knowledge. In large school systems, it is practically impossible for administrators to know every student, so their recommendations often are secondhand ones. However, in almost all cases they still have much strength.

The recommendation procedure in most schools is as follows: When the student makes application to a competitive college, he names the three teachers who know him best; they fill out anecdotal reports which emphasize specific evidence of ability, creativity, application, and personality make-up. These reports are received by the principal or director of guidance, who use them to prepare an individual description for each student. In addition, each student has received personality ratings from all his teachers at the end of his third year, and the consensus of these ratings is used to fill in blanks on the college transcript. Finally, cumulative records are reviewed, all test scores and scholastic grades are taken into account, and a recommendation is made both in terms of the student and the college he has selected.

This recommendation is made by the counselor and then reviewed by the principal or director of guidance. As a result, those making the recommendations may not know the student but are able to do a fairly effective job of recommending him to a particular college. Most schools follow this or related procedures; their intention is to help their students gain admission to the proper college.

For students who are still in the early years of high school, the aforementioned should take on added importance. While in school you are making the records that must be translated by others. Keep this in mind as you participate in activities, do your school work, and live in the society that contains other students and teachers. A few unfortunate incidents, a few unnecessary controversies, or a few mistakes during your high school days may affect the type of recommendation you receive.

There are students who must move frequently from one school to another, and many of them have unwarranted fears about how this migratory behavior will affect their chances for gaining admission to college. Either a brief note of explanation from your counselor about the different schools you attended, or your own description of your problem will increase the awareness of admissions officials about your predicament. A competent counselor can be of inestimable value to you, and the sophistication of most admissions persons would nullify any imagined deleterious effects of movement from one school to another. If you had very positive relations with the faculty at one school, there is no reason why you could not request letters of reference from these individuals and make them part of your record at the next school you attend.

FILLING OUT APPLICATIONS

The day you request an application or any information from a college marks the beginning of a file on you in most colleges. Applications submitted are read very carefully and become important factors in your acceptance or rejection. As a result, you must be very painstaking in filling out your application blank.

We would suggest that you refrain from filling in the actual blank immediately. Write your answers to the many questions on a blank sheet of paper, correct or edit them carefully, and then transfer them neatly to the official blank. Omit answers to questions when you are uncertain about their meaning or application to you, and seek the advice of your guidance counselor or one of the school's administrative officials. Underline when asked to underline, print or type when you are so requested, and write in longhand when the application tells you to do so.

Many schools request that you write an autobiographical sketch, and you should prepare this very carefully. If possible, secure the help of one of your English teachers in making necessary corrections. Most of the autobiographical requirements emphasize the same areas; once you have prepared this sketch, you may rightfully use it time and time again. If, however, different colleges request emphasis in other areas, you must edit your original copy or prepare a new one.

You will frequently be asked to give the reasons why you selected the college. You are not expected to be completely original, and a simple response will have just as much meaning as a very elaborate reply which attempts to prove your versatility in writing.

One of the most important things to be wary of when filling out application blanks is the possibility of spelling or grammatical errors. Heed instructions. Do not attempt to deceive the admissions officers by having someone else author your material. A discrepancy between your type of writing and verbal test scores may be picked up and used against you.

MAILING APPLICATIONS ON TIME

With the rash of applications and the rush of applicants to college, you will have to be very careful about meeting deadlines for application blanks. In your zeal you may act a little too hastily by sending in applications in advance of the specified opening date. Opening and closing dates will vary from college to college, and this again requires a careful reading of catalogs and announcements.

The only time we urge young people to send in applications as early as possible is when they are applying to out-of-state non-private schools. At times, these schools may be flooded with non-resident applicants and may suddenly close out such applications long before the announced closing date.

Most high school offices must handle a great number of requests for transcripts, and you therefore should assume the responsibility of getting your material into the school office long before the deadline on the application blank. Most high schools demand that students request their transcripts at least a month before an announced deadline.

ACCEPTANCE DATES

In recent years, many schools have been using a *rolling-admissions* policy, meaning that as soon as your application and test scores are in, a committee will take action and notify you of their decision in from two to six weeks. This policy has created problems for students who hope to attend prestige schools, which send out acceptance notices very late in the school year.

Colleges subscribing to rolling-admissions have found themselves being used as "insurance" schools by many students who are unsure about their chances for admission to the first-choice school. They have found themselves with many vacancies created by the failure of some students to appear for the first semester of college, and consequently, they have been forced to develop a new technique for dealing with their dilemma. Once a student has acknowledged a school's acceptance letter and has expressed his intention to attend, many institutions request deposits of from $100 to $300 within a short time. For the student whose parents can afford to forfeit this deposit if he chooses not to attend that school, this policy presents no problem. But for most students, this procedure will force them to give serious prior thought to applying and gaining acceptance at a school that is not their first choice.

There are other variations in requesting confirmation from accepted applicants. Some schools expect confirmation within one or two weeks of notification of acceptance. A number of College Board schools subscribe to the Candidates Reply Date, which is May 1st. This is the earliest date by which a candidate admitted as a freshman is required to give notice of his decision to attend that college. If you have acceptances from colleges with different confirmation dates, you will be faced with the problem of either paying the fees or taking the calculated risk of giving up the first acceptance and waiting for the second or third at a later date.

If neither of these alternatives is feasible, you might call the school that is insisting on a deposit and request an extension. Many schools have become very flexible about granting such requests. Another alternative would be to have your counselor call your first-choice college, explain your predicament, and hope that the college can give you a verbal acceptance or a statement about your admissions status. Additionally many school catalogs state that students may request special admissions notification through a written statement from their counselor.

Counselors, of course, would prefer a fixed date of acceptance notification for all schools; but until this becomes standard practice, students will continue to find themselves caught in the dilemma of having to gamble on first-choice college admissions. Perhaps the ideal way to reduce the number of multiple applications and to relieve the anxieties of the apllicants is for all schools to subscribe to the policy of rolling-admissions, combined with acceptance of the Candidate Reply Date.

EARLY ACCEPTANCE PLAN

Within the last few years, most schools have subscribed to the Early Acceptance Plan (also called the Early Decision Plan).

Colleges which subscribe to this plan agree to follow a common schedule for early decision applicants. These schools expect applications and financial aid requests by a specified date (no later than November 1st), and they agree to notify the applicant by a specified date (no later than December 1st). Early acceptance colleges may offer either a *single-choice plan* or a *first-choice plan.* Under the first-choice plan, a student may initially file applications to as many schools as he pleases. However, as soon as he is notified of acceptance by his first-choice college, he must notify all other colleges that he is withdrawing his applications.

Under the single-choice plan, the student may not apply to any other institutions until a decision has been reached on his application to the first.

For students considering the Early Acceptance Plan, SAT's and/or Achievements or ACT's should be taken in the junior year. A few schools will accept test scores taken at the beginning of the senior year, but with such a delay, you risk not getting test scores in on time.

Action taken on your request for consideration for Early Acceptance might be:

• Acceptance
• Outright rejection
• Retention of your application for possible review with all other applications at the regular time later in the school year.

Proponents of the Early Acceptance Plan argue that the number of multiple applications will be cut down considerably by the fact that some students will know their college placement by December of their senior year and will not have to undergo the stress of waiting for college acceptance. They also believe that the plan will force young people to indicate their first choices, and that once they know the school's reaction, they may be able to plan better for admission to other schools.

Those who object to this program feel that eventually most colleges will join the parade. Some will join purely to prove that they too are selective, since the original initiators of the program were mainly the very select or prestige colleges. Another objection is the belief that many students are not completely ready to make a college choice at the end of the junior year or beginning of the senior year, and as a result choose unwisely. It has also been stated that this program could easily lead to a condition under which *all* students apply for Early Acceptance, thus negating the aims of the entire procedure. Indeed, some have facetiously suggested that the end result might be an early acceptance program commencing with applications upon completion of kindergarten or the first grade of grammar school.

You should, however, give serious consideration to the Early Acceptance or Early Decision Plan, since many colleges have adopted it in some form and are steadily increasing the number of students they are admitting under this procedure. To illustrate the change in numbers, one college, which initially limited its intake under this plan to five percent of its entering class, is now admitting over one-third on this basis. Rumors abound that some fairly selective schools are admitting more than 30 percent of their freshman class through the Early Acceptance Plan.

The list of schools involved in this program has lengthened in recent years and apparently will continue to do so in the future. If certain schools are of prime interest to you, check their most recent catalogs for up-to-date information on their Early Acceptance Plans. Next, see your guidance counselor and secure his reaction to your attempt to gain admission in this fashion. If he agrees, you should be sure to follow *all* the requirements of the school to which you are applying. In the meantime, since you still may receive a rejection or a delay in action, write away for other applications, fill them out, and have them ready for distribution if and when you are notified of rejection or deferred action. Remember that this program offers you no assurances.

Remember also that for most of these schools you must take entrance tests in your junior year. Responsibility for meeting specific test requirements, deadlines, etc. is yours. Our statements about this plan pertain to most colleges and do not take into consideration individual variations.

EARLY ADMISSIONS PROGRAM

The Early Admissions Program has been in effect for many years. Its chief function has been to take very bright or gifted youngsters into college before they complete high school. Follow-up studies on graduates of this program have shown that from a group standpoint, those graduated from college under this program have done as well, if not better, than their colleagues of comparable ability who entered college after graduation from high school.

If you have any interest in this program, you should check current catalogs of schools of interest to you for their position on early admissions. The list of schools endorsing and accepting candidates under this program has increased considerably in recent years. Partially, this is because of the number of high school students who dread the prospect of facing a sterile senior year, preferring instead to get an early start on their college work. In these tumultuous days of vying for students, some colleges may have been pushed into adopting early admissions programs, resulting in a consequent lowering of admission standards. Not too long ago, a young man I counseled, who lacked units, whose grades were not too attractive, and whose SAT scores were under 500, was offered early admission by an institution that he was certain would not admit him. Fortunately, I had learned that counselors who want to survive wisely refrain from making categorical statements about admissions.

Interest on your part should stem from your being considered gifted by your teachers (not by your parents) and by your counseling or administrative staff. If you are in a school which has limited facilities, you should give greater consideration to this program. If you do elect to participate in it, you *must* recognize that you will be much younger than your fellow students and may encounter problems of social adjustment. If you feel—or you have been advised—that you are not yet "ready" for college, you would probably be wise to drop the idea. If you are in a competitive high school which offers many opportunities by the nature of its regular curriculum as well as its advanced placement and honors subject offerings, then think twice before applying for the Early Admissions Program.

At a school with which I was formerly associated, a number of students who applied to colleges under this plan were accepted. In most of these cases we saw no real need for their leaving school at the end of the junior year, because our school had been participating in the advanced placement program. Some of the college admissions officers whose schools have endorsed the Early Admissions Program have indicated that where high schools offer enough challenge, most gifted students would profit just as much by remaining in high school. We encouraged only one young man to apply for early admission, and he refused, stating that he preferred remaining with his friends and biding his time. All others who went on to college under this plan did so either at their own behest or through encouragement from their parents. We did not interfere (counselors or principals must approve participation) although we could not see any urgency in their projected plans.

There is no question in our minds that this plan has merit if used by students who are gifted and emotionally mature, are in inadequate high school situations, and have a need for greater academic challenge. It may also offer answers for restless, disenchanted, and alienated students. (See Chapter 1)

As a counselor, I am not overly happy when young people consider early admissions simply because it is the "in" thing to do or because their parents take pride in impressing their friends with this alleged honor their children have received.

APPLICATIONS AFTER REJECTIONS

Let's be realistic about one point: you may place a number of applications and be rejected by all the schools to which you have applied. However, with the changed conditions brought about by the economic crunch and other factors, the chance of rejections by all schools has diminished considerably. If all your applications are rejected, it may be your fault because you failed to accept the judgment of guidance counselors who are better equipped to recommend schools. It may also be a result of your willingness to accept free advice from your neighbors, relatives, doctors, accountants, etc. There are no laws barring people from giving advice, and apparently being an "authority" in college guidance is a simple matter. Recently a parent came in to see me about her son's gaining admission and securing a scholarship to one of the prestige colleges. She proudly informed me that the family physician had aided in the selection of the school. When I checked with the physician, he admitted that he had based his recommendation on the parent's description of her son and that he was not fully familiar with the changed admission policies of colleges.

Other experiences along these lines compel me to suggest that you listen politely to your well-intentioned advisors, then rely on the recommendations of professionally trained and qualified personnel. They will admit that they do not have all the answers and, if necessary, will refer you to other proper guides or authorities.

Rejections may still come, even if you have accepted the judgment of your guidance counselors, since their recommendations have generally been based on the actions taken by the college in previous years. Unfortunately, counselors are unable to predict with absolute certainty what certain colleges will do from year to year. This problem of foretelling what colleges will do has been complicated by the number of students who file multiple applications.

If, unfortunately, you have been rejected by all the schools to which you applied, we would recommend the following:

• Stop in at your guidance office to review with your counselor other possible applications.

• Since it may be late in the season, drop notes to the colleges to which you now expect to apply. Give them a brief picture of your academic work, subjects competed, grades achieved, class rank, ACT or CEEB scores, and the program you hope to take in college. Ask these schools if there is still an opportunity for someone with your record to put in a late application, and then request an application form.

• Consider a change in program. Some colleges may have rejected you because they did not believe that your selected program was related to your indicated abilities. An example would be that of the pre-dental student who is turned down because of low or average science grades, shortage of science and mathematics courses on his transcript, and poor test scores. A school might have granted this applicant consideration for another curriculum choice, if this second choice did not place too much emphasis on the sciences. One of the colleges that rejected you may notify you that they might reconsider your application if you agree to change your career goal. Other schools to which you make late application may grant you greater consideration when you alter your program choice.

• Carefully look over the list of junior colleges, whose admission standards tend to be somewhat more lenient than those of the four-year colleges. Apply to one or two of these, with the possibility in mind of later transferring to a four-year college.

• Use some of the aids mentioned in the next section.

COLLEGE COUNSELING SERVICES

Since there are more than 2,500 junior colleges and colleges, it becomes impossible for most counselors to have complete familiarity with all of these institutions. There are bona-fide counseling agencies which have comprehensive college information, maintain excellent files on different colleges, know the admission requirements, and can be of great assistance to you if you are searching for a college. These agencies should be used if your school system has a limited or inadequate counseling staff, or if your problems are such that the staff recommends professional help outside the school.

The fees for this type of counseling are high, but you should not let this deter you. A fee of $75 to $150, terminating in a proper selection of a school, is a small price to pay when considering how much your total education will cost. The best sources for the list of agencies would be your guidance staff, your local university admissions office, your local or state Psychological Association, your state Personnel or Guidance Association, and the International Association of Counseling Services (created by the American Personnel & Guidance Association), which issues a Directory of Approved Counseling Agencies. The latter would be, by far, the best and most convenient means of gaining assistance. Most libraries have copies of their periodically revised directory of approved counseling agencies.

You may be in an area with available private services of well-trained school counselors who have visited many colleges and placed students in schools throughout the United States for a number of years. Evidence of their competence may be secured by consultation with school officials and professional counseling organizations. Many of the certified counseling centers have a turnover in staff, and it is quite conceivable that the private-practicing school counselor may have more up-to-date information than the novice counselor or the agency member whose interests may be in other counseling areas.

Newspapers often feature advertisements offering assistance to those in need of college guidance. Some of these commercial agencies specialize in camp, private school, and college counseling, and apparently most of their income is based on commissions received from the institutions they serve. Although there is always the possibiity that one of the agencies may be offering a good service, you would be well advised to view them carefully. Properly certified agencies and counselors are bound by regulations that restrict announcements of their activities; they consider it unethical to advertise.

A recent experience added to my lack of confidence in agencies that advertise their availability for college counseling. I had recommended a particular school to a student and his parents, and within a week I had a frantic parent on the phone, questioning my selection of a college. A neighbor had recommended the use of a counseling service advertised in a New York newspaper, and this agency had advised against my choice. After calming her down by describing previous experiences with this agency (prior to this time the recommended school had received top billing by the agency but, apparently, their financial relations had been severed), I assured her that her son had an excellent chance for acceptance to the school I had listed. The final action of the college bore out my contention—the young man was accepted without any reservations.

CENTERS FOR PROBLEM CASES

At one time, several non-profit organizations operated centers to assist young people in gaining admission to college. These centers required that an applicant file a registration form and pay a small fee. The applicant would have his school send in a transcript with his personality ratings and other requested information. Applicants indicated their plans and the type of college they preferred. Colleges registered with the center would review the files and contact the applicants they believed they could serve well.

In writing to these centers for their latest literature, I discovered that, with the exception of one, they have all discontinued operation—a strong indication of the changed market for colleges. The last of the national, non-profit centers is The American College Admissions Center (1601 Walnut Street, Philadelphia, Pennsylvania 19103). In addition to placing young people in college, they also do graduate school placement and career counseling.

CHAPTER 7

COLLEGE ADMISSIONS TESTS

Tests that are administered or required by colleges for admissions purposes vary. More and more of the colleges are using the Admissions Testing Program (ATP), a service of the College Entrance Examination Board (CEEB), which includes the Scholastic Aptitude Test (SAT) and Achievement Tests (ACH), or the American College Testing Program (ACT). Most schools will allow you to substitute the SAT for the ACT or vice versa. Any substitution of scores on either test should be made only on the basis of specific directions in college catalogs or written permission from admissions officers.

There are a few schools that use other tests, but generally, if colleges do insist upon the submission of test scores, you may anticipate taking either the SAT and/or ACH, or the test offered by the American College Testing Program. If you are considered a marginal applicant for admission by some schools, you may have to undergo additional testing which might include reading tests and related English achievement tests.

POSSIBLE FUTURE DEVELOPMENTS

When the number of students entering college was increasing and young people were knocking on doors for places in schools, the standardized tests were being called for by almost all colleges. Now, since there are many openings at most colleges, attitudes about the importance of test scores have changed considerably. Some schools no longer require test scores; a number give students the option of submitting their test scores; and many schools indicate that they place less emphasis on test scores than they did previously.

Some colleges, however, believe that test scores are an effective way to screen applicants and control the performance quality of freshmen classes. Utilizing test scores in this way is effective in predicting group performance but fails to take into account individual considerations. There are many capable students who do not do well on tests, and unfortunately for them, gaining admission to very selective colleges will continue to be difficult.

Speaking realistically, your scholarship opportunities also will be affected by your admissions tests scores. Some admissions officials may minimize the effects of these scores on applications for scholarships, but there have been many instances of students' weak test scores hurting their chances for scholarships.

AMERICAN COLLEGE TESTING PROGRAM (ACT)

The ACT, which was organized in 1959, has steadily increased in its adoption by institutions of higher education, scholarships agencies, and state educational systems. At the present time, 2,400 institutions or scholarships agencies either recommend or require this test. The vast majority of schools utilizing ACT are located in the South, Southwest, Midwest, and Rocky Mountain areas. There are also schools along the Eastern Seaboard and West Coast that are using the ACT. Check college catalogs to see if any school in which you are interested requires it.

The *ACT Assessment Program,* which was recently introduced, is a comprehensive program for students consisting of a battery of a battery of four tests. This three-hour (approximately) examination is divided equally among the areas of English, mathematics, social studies, and the natural sciences. The English test places emphasis on appropriateness and effectiveness of written expression (English usage). The mathematics test combines general mathematics, reasoning ability, and formal mathematics skills. The social studies and natural sciences tests examine a student's ability to read, reason, and do problem-solving. Standard scores are reported on a scale ranging from 0 to 36 points, and students are given their percentile rank in terms of national norms and also as related to college-bound populations.

The *Student Profile Section* collects admissions/enrollment data, academic and out-of-class information about the student's high school achievement, high school class work, biographical data, and self-reported high school grades in four general areas.

The *ACT Interest Inventory* is designed to measure six major interest dimensions and is used as an instrument to help students select college majors.

Your Student Profile Report, which is issued to test participants, does an excellent job of explaining what ACT scores mean, what they measure, and how they will be used. We hope that if you participate in this testing program you will take the time to utilize this booklet to advantage.

The publishers of the ACT recommend taking their tests only once, either in the junior or senior year. I question this. Students taking these tests might find it advantageous to have a trial experience, since practice may increase their scores. If a student has an "off" day when taking the test for the first time, a second trial may give a better indication of his potential.

COLLEGE ENTRANCE EXAMINATION BOARDS (CEEB)

The College Entrance Examination Board is an organization— located in Princeton, New Jersey—whose most widely-known service is the publication and administering of a number of tests used by thousands of American colleges and universities in judging applicants for admission.

The Admissions Testing Program (ATP) offered by the CEEB is of two types—the Scholastic Aptitude Test (SAT) and Achievement Tests (ACH). There is also a Test of Standard Written English, now in experimental use. It is a thirty-minute exercise in writing skills which will be used by colleges to assess students and place them in freshman English courses.

The Scholastic Aptitude Test attempts to discover a student's potential academic ability in the verbal and mathematics areas. These are considered the most important and are required more often by colleges. Remember, they seek only to determine your ability to learn in an academic situation.

The Achievement Tests are used to find out how much you have learned and how well you reason in specific subject fields. Colleges may require you to take some of these tests shortly before entrance to their schools. Requirements will vary from one test to three, with most requesting that you take the achievement tests in the field of English composition and two other subject areas relating to your program in college. Some colleges require taking the Language Achievement Test for placement. Most engineering schools which demand the Achievement Tests for admissions purposes expect you to take the Advanced Mathematics Test and either Physics or Chemistry in addition to the English Composition Test.

As you select schools, be very careful about checking their requirements and be certain that you take the required and recommended Achievement Tests. You may secure specific test requirements by reading the latest catalog of the college or by referring to an up-to-date edition of *The College Handbook,* published by the College Entrance Examination Board.

Most colleges prefer that you take your SAT's and Achievement Tests before Feburary 1st of your senior year. Students planning to attend schools that require Achievement Tests would be well advised to take them as soon as they have completed a particular subject. For example, if you have taken biology in your sophomore year, you should take the Achievement Test in this subject long before your senior year. If you complete intermediate algebra at the end of your junior year and do not plan to continue with mathematics, take this Achievement Test, if required by one of your college choices, as early as possible. If you are considering the Early Acceptance or Early Admission Plan, remember to check college catalogs for the recommended dates for taking the various tests.

With the widespread use of the Preliminary Scholastic Aptitude Test (PSAT), which is given in October of each year, the College Entrance Examination Board expects juniors to take this test for practice purposes. The Board does not recommend taking the SAT again for practice, but we cannot, in good faith, go along with this suggestion in all cases. Since high school counselors are using these tests to assist you in the selection of a college, and since colleges visited during your junior year might use these scores in showing either a favorable or unfavorable reaction to your forthcoming application, it sometimes is wise to check the reliability of the PSAT by taking the SAT for practice purposes in your junior year. Your counselor is the best judge of your need to take practice SAT's. If you believe that your PSAT scores do not match your academic record and that they are not indicative of your potential, consider taking the SAT for still further practice.

Although I am not partial to taking tests, and despite the reduced emphasis on test scores, you would be well advised to take your SAT's several times, until you achieve a score 30 to 50 points above your PSAT's. If you are applying to a very selective school, with five to ten applicants for each opening, the importance of good SAT or ACT scores cannot be minimized. I urge students to take admissions tests several times because of the variations of scores from one date to another. There are drops in

There is decreasing emphasis on entrance and I.Q. examinations as counselors realize the importance of a student's academic background.

scores and there are marked elevations in the results. Many colleges take the highest set or the highest in each section in evaluating your credentials.

If you are unable to take the PSAT, do not hesitate to take some SAT's during your junior year. If the PSAT is available, even if you are undecided about going on to college, take the test anyhow. There is no limit on the number of times you may take the SAT's, and there *is* some practice effect, as evidenced by a major study conducted by the CEEB.

To the best of my knowledge, colleges do not penalize applicants for taking any set of tests several times. However, when taking entrance examinations for graduate or professional schools, there are some law schools, for example, that average your scores in considering your application. Other professional schools may follow this same policy, and it might be wise to check the practices of graduate schools to which you expect to apply.

USE OF PRACTICE BOARDS

Taking the Practice Boards, or exposure to the PSAT, offers many advantages. It gives you and your school an opportunity to predict what your future scores on the College Boards may be. It also helps you and your school to consider prospective colleges with a greater degree of accuracy when College Boards are required. It helps you personally, because there is a practice effect which will show itself, in most cases, by a slight increase in your test scores. From a psychological standpoint, experiencing the PSAT or practice Boards may help you so that your second experience may find you less tense.

Students ask us whether these Board scores may be used against them, since on occasion they may not do well on their practice Boards. Colleges may secure your practice scores on the PSAT through your school. All colleges do not ask for these practice Boards, but during your visits to schools a question may be asked about your scores on these tests.

At the present time CEEB forwards to the schools you designate every set of scores. This is done for your advantage, since a previous set may be better than a more recent one, and you might want the college to see the earlier scores. If your early scores are particularly poor this will not harm you, since most colleges will consider the better of two sets of scores. Some colleges will take the highest in each area.

It is wise to keep a record of the tests that you have taken, the dates on which you have taken them, and the results. You will then be able to make requests that will facilitate the services of the CEEB in forwarding test results to colleges.

MEANING AND SIGNIFICANCE OF SCORES

Recently the Admissions Testing Program of the College Entrance Examination Board issued booklets entitled *About the*

SAT and *About the Achievement Tests,* which are given to each student at the time he receives his test scores. These booklets are available in your guidance office, and they should be read very carefully. They are valuable because College Board scores are subject to a tremendous amount of misinterpretation by students. You should understand that scores may range from 200 to 800, and there is no such thing as failing this test. Your test scores place you in a relative position, comparing your aptitudes and achievements to other students throughout the country.

Today a verbal aptitude score of 435 and a math aptitude score of 475 generally place you in the 50th percentile of all those going on to college. This means that you have done better than 50 percent of the students taking this test, and conversely, 50 percent have done better than you. The 50th percentile does not imply that you secured a score of 50 or that you got 50 percent of your answers correct. A score of 395 or thereabouts would place you in the 31st percentile. This would indicate that you have done better than over 30 percent of the students taking the test (this is a positive approach), or that 69 percent have done better than you.

Notwithstanding the excellent interpretation of the meaning and significance of your scores in the booklets, most students achieving scores around 450 describe themselves as stupid, inept, etc. They base their evaluations on a comparison with friends or top students who have done exceedingly well on the tests. Remember that if all seniors, noncollege as well as collegebound, took these tests, the average verbal score would run around 345.

The advice given by the booklets should be heeded. Test scores have too often been misinterpreted by students, and the task of using them in the context of college admissions is both difficult and complex. You should consult your guidance counselor and the admissions officers of colleges to help you interpret and apply the scores to the question of your chances of gaining admission.

USES OF REGULAR BOARDS BY COLLEGES

Colleges view test scores as an additional screening device. Profiles of even the most selective schools will show acceptances of a small percentage of students with scores running from 400 up. However, a preponderance of the accepted students in these selective schools will have SAT's of over 600. Cutoff points on these tests vary. Some schools will respect above-average class rank and overlook weak College Board scores; whereas others will place greater emphasis on these test results. At the present time scores of 450 or above will allow you to gain admission to over 90 percent of the colleges if your grades, personality ratings, and recommendations are acceptable.

Strong College Boards will stand you in good stead if your academic record is not too convincing. There are colleges that will be willing to grant you an opportunity if your College Boards are what they consider presentable, meaning scores of 400, 450, 500, or thereabouts—again depending on the school. There is no need to despair if you have not achieved scores that you consider to be good ones. Let your counselors decide what effect your test results will have on gaining admission to various colleges. If they are not certain, let the college itself accept or reject you.

TUTORING AND OTHER AIDS

The Admissions Testing Program of the College Entrance Examination Board has publicized the results of several major studies on the possible effect on SAT scores of coaching or private tutoring. Its first study concerned itself with students in private schools and statistically found no evidence of any significant differences between those who were coached and those who were not. The second study used high school students of equal ability for control and experimental groups. This study corroborated the previous study, with a slight difference in the effects on the Mathematics Aptitude section.

A third study used individual coaching with selected control and experimental groups, and this too minimized the effect of coaching on the test results. The studies did indicate one thing that might prove of value to most schools and students. Seniors not taking mathematics tended to drop or remain stationary in the Mathematics Aptitude portion of the SAT. This in itself should suggest that you review, with the aid of your school staff or by yourself, eighth grade arithmetic and elementary algebra. Such a review may help you to avoid a drop in your scores. Other studies reported in professional journals in recent years have confirmed previously announced results.

Many books promising to help you prepare for these tests have been published. No harm will befall you if you review the material in these books, although the latest brochure sent to you by the College Entrance Examination Board at the time of registration is considered of sufficient value to you in practicing for the test.

In addition to the books promising to help improve your scores, a number of coaching schools advertise their services. Some make extravagant promises by publishing only the scores of students taking their course who improved considerably, but not listing those who either dropped or retained their original scores. A few school systems have also been making it a practice to operate coaching classes for their students. Not too long ago a local adult school made available its facilities for coaching students for the College Boards. At the termination of the course there was no significant difference between the "before and after" averages beyond the expected increase based on practice and maturation.

You and your parents should realize that the aptitude tests are based on cumulative experience, and it is virtually impossible to develop a respectable vocabulary or verbal ability in two or three months of tutoring. By the same token, it is highly improbable that you could dramatically improve your mathematical aptitude in a short period of time.

Insofar as the Achievement Tests are concerned, there is no question in our minds about the possible advantages of coaching and tutoring. Since these tests are based on actual accomplishments in subject areas, you can review the subject material and should be able to elevate your scores considerably. We recommend that all our students spend some time reviewing for the Achievement Tests and even suggest that they secure outside help if they have been away from the specific subject area for a period of time. Many private schools, and some public schools, offer special review classes for the different subjects.

Summing up, you would be wise at the beginning of high school to work on the building of a vocabulary and concentrate on your mathematics, with occasional review sessions of basic arithmetic. *(Incidentally, by far the strongest way of building verbal aptitudes and vocabulary is NOT by studying lists of words but by constant and continued reading in all types of mature literature. This cannot be begun too soon.)*

It would also be sensible for you to carefully review the material published by the Admissions Testing Program of the College Entrance Examination Board to assist you in preparation for these tests. You might also consider borrowing books that promise to help you prepare for the tests, as long as you do not expect miracles. If you have test-taking sessions available in your school, you may be helped somewhat by conditioning yourself to this type of test and the testing situation, by picking up a few basic tricks and techniques of taking tests, and by reviewing some basic mathematics.

If you must take the Achievement Tests, by all means volunteer for review classes offered by your school, study by yourself, or spend money on tutorial help to aid you in increasing your scores. The first two methods should prove more effective since they are based on self-motivation, which is far more productive than the last in effecting better test results.

CHAPTER 8

SCHOLARSHIPS AND FINANCIAL AID

There are several popular myths and misconceptions associated with scholarships and financial aid. These distortions, and the reasons why they are invalid, need to be explored before we delve into a detailed discussion of how to get help in paying for your college education. Some of the most common myths are:

• *There is a possibility of scholarship assistance for all who require it.*

A beautiful fantasy, promoted by publications that predicate sales on promises that cannot be kept. Optimistic speakers complicate counselors' existences by their repeating the myth that financial help is the easiest thing in the world to secure. There is partial truth in this statement, to the extent that approximately 1/3 of the eligible needy have failed to take advantage of available financial assistance; however, gathering the aid and putting it all together is far from a simple task.

• *If you search hard and long enough through source material, you will discover some very unusual scholarships.*

Unusual scholarships do exist, and finding the one that might fit a specific student's situation is comparable to looking for a needle in a haystack. Exhaustive searching can help in locating sources of possible assistance; however, as a general rule, this procedure discloses very specialized scholarships for a select group of students. For example, one scholarship is available to any student whose name is Kelly, who lives in New Haven, Connecticut, and who qualifies for admission to Yale. There are many others which are equally specialized and which will probably go unclaimed for many more years.

• *For a small fee, computers can give you access to many scholarships.*

Many students have employed computer sources without securing adequate and meaningful scholarship lists. Many of these services are deceptive and ineffective because the lists they produce lack relevancy for the individual student. They do not give adequate details about the academic expectations of the scholarship donors, nor do they provide an accurate picture of the number of competitors. If we could gather all information relative to scholarship and financial aid, feed it into the machine, and take into consideration the many variables related to assistance, computerized scholarship lists might be useful. However, by the time this could be accomplished, additions, deletions, and corrections would make some of the information out-of-date.

• *Only needy or bright, gifted students can receive financial assistance.*

Most forms of financial assistance *are* awarded on the basis of proven financial need or in recognition of academic excellence. However, there are some "no-need" scholarships available (discussed later in this chapter), and diligent research in up-to-date information sources in your guidance counselor's office should turn up some financial aid programs for which students of average means and ability will qualify.

FEDERAL ASSISTANCE

In 1965, the Higher Education Act was passed to financially assist students in post-secondary and higher education institutions. Since implementation of the Act, many modifications have been made to it, and at present, there are five federal financial aid programs supported by the United States Office of

Education. The discussion which follows is up-to-date as it is published; however, you should keep in mind that federal programs are subject to change and for the most current data, you should check government literature.

THE BASIC EDUCATIONAL OPPORTUNITY
GRANT (BEOG) PROGRAM

This program makes available funds to eligible students attending approved or accredited colleges, vocational schools, technical institutes, and schools of nursing, as well as other post-high school institutions. It is an entitlement program, with eligibility decisions made through the United States Office of Education. Any student who began college, vocational school, etc. after a specified date (for the academic year 1975-1976 the date is April 1, 1973) may apply by completing a form called "Application for Determination of Basic Grant Eligibility." Copies are available at many public libraries or may be secured by writing: P.O. Box 84, Washington, D.C. 20044. Within four weeks after forwarding an application, students will receive notification of their eligibility. The school, or schools, to which you intend to apply will calculate the amount of the basic grant you are eligible to receive. The amount may vary with the cost of attendance at different schools.

NATIONAL DIRECT STUDENT LOAN
(NDSL) PROGRAM

These loans allow you to borrow up to a total of:
- $2,500 if you are enrolled in a vocational program or if you have completed less than two years of a program leading to a bachelor's degree

- $5,000 if you are an undergraduate student who has completed only two years of study toward a bachelor's degree
- $10,000 for graduate study.

The latter two sums include any amount you borrowed under NDSL for previous schooling. Repayment of these loans begins nine months after leaving or graduating from school, and you are allowed up to ten years to pay back the total amount. The interest rate is three percent on the unpaid balance of the loan principal. There are special provisions for loan cancellation for borrowers who go into certain fields of teaching or specialized military duty.

One interesting aspect of this loan program is that its funds are made available to both full- and part-time (at least half-time) students. Apply for NDSL loans through the financial aid officer at your school. Determination of need is made by the individual institution, using an Office of Education approved need analysis.

SUPPLEMENTAL EDUCATIONAL OPPORTUNITY GRANT (SEOG) PROGRAM

This program is dedicated to students who would not be able to continue their education without a grant. Recipients must be in exceptional financial need and must be enrolled at least half-time as undergraduate or professional students in approved institutions. Again, your college financial aid officer is responsible for determining whether you will receive a grant and the amount that will be awarded. At present, the grant cannot be less than $200 or more than $1,500 a year, and it normally may be reissued for four years. If you are selected for an SEOG, the awarding institution must provide you with additional financial aid at least equal to the amount granted you through SEOG.

COLLEGE WORK-STUDY (CWS) PROGRAM

This program provides positions for students who have financial need and must earn part of their educational expenses. Applications can be made through your school's financial aid officer if you are enrolled at least half-time in an approved post-secondary educational institution through graduate school. If you are eligible, you may be employed as many as forty hours a week; the job and the hours that you may work are determined by the financial aid officer. The financial aid officer will consider your need, school schedule, health, and academic progress.

GUARANTEED STUDENT LOAN PROGRAM

This program enables prospective students to borrow directly from banks, credit unions, savings and loan associations, or other lenders who are willing to make loans to students. These loans are guaranteed by a state or private non-profit agency or insured by the federal government. Those students who are enrolled at least half-time in an eligible college or university, a school of nursing, or a vocational, technical training, business, or home study school may apply for a loan. The amount that students may borrow varies, depending upon the state in which they reside, but the maximum loan total is $2,500 per year, with an interest rate of not more than seven percent. The total amount for undergraduate or vocational study is $7,500; for graduate study alone, or in combination with undergraduate study, the total that may be borrowed is $10,000. This loan program should be of particular interest to middle-income families, since they may be eligible for federal interest benefits, which postpone interest until loan repayment begins. If adjusted family income (the amount of income on which income tax is paid) is less than $15,000, a family automatically qualifies for interest subsidy on loans up to

$2,000 per year. For interest subsidy on a loan that is larger than $2,000, you must secure a recommendation from your school to forward to the lender. This recommendation is a determination by the school on how much a student actually needs to continue his or her education. This need analysis takes into account the cost of the education and the family's ability to pay for it. If adjusted family income is $15,000 or more, and you wish to apply for an interest subsidy on a loan of any amount, you should request a recommendation from your school, again based on a need analysis.

The Guaranteed Student Loan Program requires that all monies be used for educational purposes and must be repaid in full, with payments beginning nine to twelve months after leaving or graduating from school. You may take up to ten years to repay the loan, with the amount of payments determined by the size of the debt. A minimum payment of $360 a year is required.

Additional information and application forms are available from schools, lenders, State Guarantee Agencies, and regional offices of the United States Office of Education. Brochures issued by the United States Department of Health, Education, and Welfare list sources of information on the Guaranteed Student Loan Program.

This loan program is one of the best financial aids for middle-income families. Because repayment is deferred until after graduation, the student can help clear the debt with his increased earnings.

NATIONAL MERIT SCHOLARSHIP PROGRAM

This scholarship program is by far the largest and best developed financial resource for bright and outstanding young people. When the scholarship corporation was created in 1955, most of its grants came from the Ford Foundation. Today, however, over 550 corporations, foundations, professional associations, unions, trusts, and colleges are involved in the program, which offers over 4,200 Merit and Special scholarships. A related program, the National Achievement Scholarship Program for Outstanding Negro Students, has also enjoyed phenomenal growth in sponsor participation, with 135 organizations and donors supporting almost 500 Achievement Scholarships per year. Both these programs are administered by the National Merit Scholarship Corporation (NMSC).

The NMSC conducts the Preliminary Scholastic Aptitude Test/National Merit Scholarship Qualifying Test (PSAT/NMSQT), which is taken by secondary school students as the first step in the annual competition. Students competing for scholarships or for recognition must be United States citizens (or planning to obtain citizenship), be enrolled as full-time secondary school students, plan to attend a regionally accredited United States college, and take this test at the proper time in their high school program. Scheduling details for students who plan to leave high school before their twelfth year or graduate in three years may be culled from the latest PSAT/NMSQT bulletin.

Those placing in the top two percent of the nation's graduating high school seniors will be designated Commended Students and will receive letters of commendation. These Commended Students, who will be designated in the fall of their senior year, are asked to report their first and second choice colleges to NMSC, which will send their names and test scores to the colleges, without giving the order of school preference. NMSC will also make the names and home addresses of Commended Students available for institutions interested in enrolling high-scoring students. Each year, approximately 35,000 participants become Commended Students.

About 15,000 top-scoring students whose Selection Index Scores qualify them as Semi-Finalists continue in the competition for merit scholarships. Their scores (twice the verbal added to the mathematics aptitude) place them in the top one half of one percent of the high school seniors. As with the Commended Students, the Semi-Finalists' first and second choice colleges will receive reports of their Merit Program standing. To become Finalists, the Semi-Finalists must meet the following qualifications:

• Must be enrolled full time in their final year of secondary school, with plans to enter a regionally accredited United States college in the fall after graduation. (Exception is made for the student who spends three years or less in grades nine through twelve);

• Must have maintained high academic standing, with documentation of the academic record (if enrolled in college, an official transcript must be submitted);

• Must be fully endorsed and recommended by the secondary school principal;

• Must complete the scholarship application sent through their secondary school;

• Must confirm the PSAT/NMSQT scores by an equivalent performance on the Scholastic Aptitude Test of the Admissions Testing Program of the College Entrance Examination Board by early November.

About 90 percent of the Semi-Finalists attain Finalist standing in each Merit Qualifying Competition. Semi-Finalists are asked, but not required, to provide NMSC with confidential family financial information. The NMSC uses this information to determine the annual stipend of those Finalists chosen to receive a corporate-sponsored, four-year merit scholarship.

There are three types of merit scholarships awarded in each competition. The National Merit $1,000 scholarships are awarded each year to at least 1,000 Finalists, with distribution by state or special selection unit. In making these selections, a Selection Committee considers the academic record, two sets of test scores, leadership qualities, extra-curricular interests, accomplishments, recommendations, and characterization of the student, as well as the student's own statements. These one-time awards of $1,000 are underwritten by business and industrial sponsors.

About 1,300 renewal awards for up to four years of college undergraduate study are offered annually by corporations, foundations, professional associations, unions, and trusts. These corporation-sponsored scholarships have particular qualifications, with a great deal of emphasis on children of employees or members of the sponsoring organization, those residing in the area or communities where a corporation has operations, or those planning selected fields of study. The determination of the awards is the responsibility of NMSC; however, sponsors require students to submit entry blanks to the corporation. The stipends normally range from $250 to $1,500 per year for up to four years of study. The awards take into account the financial information submitted and the cost data of the college of the student's choice.

There are now about 1,500 renewable Merit Scholarships sponsored by accredited United States colleges and universities. These institutions choose their winners from among the Finalists who plan to attend their schools, and they determine the stipend amounts for their winners. These awards are based on the need-analysis procedures and reporting services of either the College Scholarship Service (CSS) or the American College Testing Program (ACT). The colleges may also add loans and employment as well as the scholarship assistance. The scholarship stipend must represent at least half the senior's computed need, with limits of $100 minimum and $1,500 maximum.

There are also about 130 corporations and business organizations that sponsor Special Scholarships. They have awarded as many as 475 four-year scholarships to children of employees or students residing in communities where the corporation operates. These corporations distribute entry blanks and NMSC decides the winners. The applicants must have high PSAT/NMSQT scores (however, below the scores of the Merit Semi-Finalists); awards are administered in the same fashion as the Merit Scholarships. The names of these winners are not published.

NATIONAL ACHIEVEMENT SCHOLARSHIP PROGRAM FOR OUTSTANDING NEGRO STUDENTS

This program seeks to assist academically able black high school students in gaining college admission and receiving financial aid. Black students who enter the Merit Program may simultaneously enter the Achievement Program, but their test performance is evaluated independently of the Merit Programs. In recent years, about 3,000 eligible black students were designated as Commended Students, and the roster listing their names was submitted to colleges and universities. At the same time, labels with their names and addresses were also made available to regionally accredited United States colleges.

About 1,500 black students who qualify as Achievement Program Semi-Finalists are considered for Finalist status to qualify for the scholarships. Awards in this program include National Achievement $1,000 Scholarships, corporation-sponsored, four-year Achievement Scholarships, and college-sponsored, four-year Achievement Scholarships. The PSAT and NMSQT Student Bulletin lists the sponsors of the various scholarships.

OTHER SCHOLARSHIP OPPORTUNITIES

Among the other major national scholarship opportunities are the programs conducted by the Naval Reserve Officers Training corps (NROTC), the Air Force Reserve Training Corps

(AFROTC), and the Westinghouse Corporation. While Westinghouse stimulates a tremendous amount of interest in scientific exploration, they offer relatively few scholarships.

The NROTC is an ideal way of combining college and preparation to become a naval officer after graduation. Acceptance under this plan provides you with four years of education, special allowances, and a nominal salary each month while in school. To qualify, you must take the special examinations which are conducted once a year, be accepted at a college which offers this program (the NROTC booklet gives all of this information), and then meet other requirements set up by the Navy. One major disadvantage of getting an education under this scholarship program is the amount of time at college that is dedicated to subjects prescribed by the Navy and taught by naval personnel. The AFROTC also offers many four-year scholarships.

The Coast Guard and the Maritime Academy have comparable programs. Information about their offerings may be secured in your guidance office or through your library.

The Air Force, Army, and Naval Academies offer free four-year programs for prospective officers in their branches of the service. If you are interested in attending one of the service academies, you should investigate their admission requirements before the end of your junior year in high school. You should keep in mind that the primary purpose of these federal academies is to prepare career officers and not merely to be a means of free financing of a collegiate education.

In past years, a number of industrial concerns and foundations conducted their own scholarship programs. Recently there has been a trend to have colleges administer the scholarships and select the recipients. Among the groups now using this approach are General Motors, Union Carbide, Proctor and Gamble, Western Electric, and the Alfred P. Sloan National Scholarship program. Details about these programs may be secured in your guidance office or by writing directly to colleges.

STATE REHABILITATION COMMISSIONS

One should not overlook the possibility of obtaining financial aid through State Rehabilitation Commissions. With federal assistance, many such organizations have developed programs to aid people at all levels in receiving training commensurate with their potential. Their objective is to assist individuals with physical or emotional problems in becoming self-supporting. Applications are forwarded through physicians or schools, or are self-initiated. The Commission arranges for psychological or physical evaluations and then decides whether the applicant comes within the range of those they will assist. There is a considerable amount of red tape to endure, but there is always the possibility of assistance, most of which is not based on financial need. Throughout the years, I have managed to help at least two people per year to obtain college or post-high school training financial aid through this program.

NOTE TO PARENTS: If your child has been treated for an emotional problem or has any type of physical disability (asthma, back trouble, auditory problems, polio, etc.), secure the address of your nearest Rehabilitation Commission Center. Call the supervisor and request advice on filing an application. If the professional at the agency cannot give you a definitive response, he will most likely urge you to file an application. (In New Jersey, it is imperative for applicants to have filed for a state scholarship, whether or not they believe they are entitled to assistance.)

STATE AND OTHER SCHOLARSHIP HELP

By the time this book is published, almost all states will be offering some type of scholarship assistance to graduates within their boundaries. Despite the fact that these programs receive a great deal of publicity and are excellent sources of financial aid, invariably many students fail to secure this help. Their failure is based on one of several factors: forgetting to meet deadlines, failing to take the appropriate tests, and neglecting to submit requested financial statements.

If information about these scholarships is not available in your school's guidance office, contact your State Department of Education for detailed information about their requirements. Most states also offer loan assistance; information on this should be available in your guidance office.

There are a number of aids for war orphans and children of veterans. The Veterans Administration provides most students in this category with the necessary information on how to apply for financial assistance. Check first with the Veterans Administration for the most recent legislation offering assistance to war orphans and children of veterans, then consider contacting local veterans' organizations. A number of them, such as the American Legion, Veterans of Foreign Wars, Disabled Veterans, and Amvets, have their own scholarship programs.

AID THROUGH PROFESSIONAL ORGANIZATIONS

Most professional groups (accountants, chemists, nurses, social workers, etc.) have scholarship programs for prospective entrants into their fields. If you have definitely decided on a career in a specific field, contact the appropriate national organization for scholarship information. The simplest and easiest way to secure addresses of organizations is through the Occupational Outlook Handbook, available in practically every library and guidance office. Immediately after the descriptive occupational material, they list affiliated organizations with their addresses. A card or a note to these will secure scholarship information and other career material.

EVALUATING SCHOLARSHIP NEEDS

Who should apply for a scholarship and how colleges determine financial need are questions frequently asked of guidance counselors. To answer this question, we recommend to parents and students that they sit down with pencil and paper and work out a balance sheet with estimated school costs for the year and possible income from all sources. This income, which should include your present savings, should be prorated for four years, or longer if you contemplate graduate school. You should also attempt to estimate your potential earnings for summer work. After adding the amount that your parents are able to give you, if you still do not have sufficient money to cover tuition and board (if attending school away from home) or tuition (if attending school at home), then you are justified in requesting scholarship help. Financial need will not assure you of a scholarship, but if you have achieved a good academic record in high school and there is indicated need, opportunities for scholarship help should be good.

It is a mistaken notion that assistance is given only to top scholars, and a perusal of any chart with distribution of scholarship aid to applicants on the basis of class rank and/or SAT/ACT scores will readily dispel this idea. A preponderance of aid will invariably go to the better scholars, but remember, "nothing ventured, nothing gained." Colleges have their own methods of evaluating financial need. They may refuse to accept your judgment by either cutting down your request or flatly refusing to grant you help, or they may grant you assistance. *Let the financial aid officers at the different schools make the decision.*

If you apply for scholarship help to a college which subscribes to the ACT or CEEB Scholarship or Financial Aid Services, secure one of their application blanks, have it filled out by your parents, and use it as a guide for determining the amount of money you need. Copies of financial aid blanks are available in every guidance office. Otherwise write to College Scholarship Service, Box 176, Princeton, N.J. 08540 or Box 1501, Berkeley, California 94701, or to ACT Student Need Analysis Service, P.O. Box 767, Iowa City, Iowa 52240.

VARYING ATTITUDES ON NEED

Need is apparently estimated and defined in various ways by colleges. Heavily endowed schools with ample funds may be more liberal in making awards than schools with limited pocketbooks. Different criteria are used to determine need for help, and this makes it extremely difficult to establish a set rule for determining when to make scholarship awards. Some schools have granted scholarship help to students when family incomes have exceeded $25,000. Awards in these situations may have been granted for such reasons as: there were a number of other students in the family attending college; there may have been heavy indebtedness created by the prolonged illness of a member of the family; or family obligations may have included responsibilities of caring for relatives. Commuter colleges may set $8,000-$10,000 as the income beyond which no scholarship help will be awarded.

Individual schools and agencies use their own formulas to evaluate financial need. One rule they often employ, which is far from infallible, is to estimate the family's annual income tax payment as a measure of the amount of money to be contributed for a student's college education each year. In our contacts with parents who express a desire for scholarship help, we use a pamphlet, *Meeting College Costs: A Guide for Parents and Students,* published by the College Scholarship Service of the College Entrance Examination Board. A worksheet in this brochure outlines step-by-step the needs analysis the College Scholarship Service uses to determine what parents can reasonably be expected to pay toward educational expenses. By going through this worksheet item by item, a family can find out roughly what amount the colleges may expect from them. This estimation is not as precise as the evaluation made by a college on the basis of information provided in the Parents' Confidential Statement or the Family Financial Statement. If the figure for your expected contribution seems high, keep in mind that colleges may arrange extended payments or can recommend agencies that have financing plans.

American College Testing Program has established the ACT Student Need Analysis Service to help students applying for financial aid. Like the College Scholarship Service, it arranges for the filing of a Family Financial Statement. The Comprehensive Financial Aid Report then generates an estimated financial need for the student. Filing for assistance through the BEOG program is another method of securing some determination of a student's financial need. Action on these applications is taken within a four-week period, and students are advised of the amount of assistance they will receive when accepted at different schools.

In considering applications for aid, parents and students might keep in mind the fundamental principles on which colleges participating in the College Scholarship Service agree. Briefly summarized, the main points are as follows:

• Assistance is provided to students who would otherwise be unable to attend a particular college.

• Assistance is defined as scholarships, grants, loans, and employment.

• Families are expected to assume the major financial burden, and colleges should be expected only to supplement the effort of the family.

• In the selection of students to receive assistance, the emphasis is placed upon their academic achievement, character, and future promise.

138　*Planning Your College Education*

• Financial assistance offered to any student by the college or other sources should not exceed the amount of money needed.

• Students requiring financial aid are expected to provide a reasonable part of the total amount to meet costs by accepting employment, or a loan, or both.

The procedure followed by most colleges in making awards is to prorate the money allocated for scholarship among the top candidates. The very best candidates may get more direct monetary aid; whereas those whose records are not as strong may secure a greater amount of assistance through loans and grants-in-aid. When the awards available through these sources are used up, the students lower on the ladder are notified that scholarship help is not available.

Again, we would suggest that, if you and your family believe that you must have some financial help, and if your grades are above average, you should make application for assistance. Counselors can tell you that over 95 percent of the scholarships are given to aid needy students in securing a higher education, not to give academic recognition. (Some parents who are not faced with financial problems have their sons and daughters apply for scholarships merely because they would like to have the recognition accorded a scholarship winner.)

"NO NEED" SCHOLARSHIPS

Many colleges and universities offer a few scholarships which are not based on need to outstanding academic students. These scholastic awards are comparable to athletic scholarships, which are granted mainly on the basis of exceptional athletic ability. One example is Washington University in St. Louis, Missouri, which has at least eight scholarships that are awarded to students of outstanding scholastic achievement, without regard to financial need. Recipients may receive as much as $10,000 for four years of study. The University of Rochester gives a number of $500 per year awards. Cass and Birmbaum's *Counselors' Comparative Guide to American Colleges* has a listing of innumerable colleges throughout the country that award a few scholarships on the basis of academic merit and/or make available special loans to middle-income students. This reference book may be available in your guidance office.

If you have a good academic record, you might consider writing to colleges for information on special honorary scholarships. These "no need" scholarships were the subject of an article in the College Board Review, in which the author noted that the number of colleges granting such awards was much higher than suspected.

EFFECTS OF SCHOLARSHIP APPLICATIONS

One of the questions frequently raised by students and parents is the treatment of their scholarship applications by colleges. Some are fearful that a rejection for scholarship aid will automatically carry along with it refusal of admission. This is true in only a very few instances.

Many colleges separate their scholarship awards from their admissions policies. Under this division of duties, even if you are denied scholarship aid, you receive notice of acceptance if the school considers you a worthy applicant. When schools follow this practice, you do not have to worry about the effect scholarship requests will have on admissions.

In general, most schools do not allow your application for a scholarship to interfere with your chances for admission. If you are more eager for acceptance at a college than you are for scholarship help, and you believe that your scholarship application might affect your admissions status, you might withhold applying for assistance. A number of schools are now making it a practice to give more awards after the freshman year, allocating funds for students who have proven their ability to do college work.

There are some moral issues involved in making applications for scholarships. Some schools may refuse you admission because of your apparent inability to finance your education. If they cannot assure you of scholarship assistance, they may be fearful that your financial situation might weigh you down and affect your academic achievement. In making this judgment, they are taking you at your word when you contend that you must have financial assistance to continue your education. On the other hand, many students contradict their statements of financial need by giving up a scholarship to a lesser school to attend a more selective college without any financial help. There is a temptation here to be critical of those making this type of shift; however, sometimes the advantages of a more selective academic setting, despite the possible financial burden, far outweigh the disadvantages.

APPLYING FOR A SCHOLARSHIP

Many students come into our office to ask how they may apply for scholarship aid. In most cases, the request should be made directly to the college, asking for both the types of scholarships available and for application forms. If the college is a member of the CEEB or ACT Scholarship Service, it may forward the necessary papers that must be completed and returned; forms may also be picked up in the guidance office. Great care should be taken in filling out applications—statements should be checked very carefully and then re-checked to make sure that everything has been filled out accurately and properly. Once financial details have been submitted (a copy should be kept), parents should be ready to discuss any statements if they are interviewed by a representative of the college. Permission to allow colleges to secure copies of income tax statements is now requested by most scholarship services.

SECURING SCHOLARSHIP HELP

One of the counselor's most difficult and unpleasant tasks is convincing parents and students that despite the tremendous amount of publicity, there still is not enough scholarship aid for most above-average students who are worthy of a college education. A number of books and magazine articles have been published in recent years stressing the unused scholarships which have not been picked up and suggesting that these can be garnered with a show of resourcefulness. There is no question that some scholarships are not picked up, and there is no doubt about the failure of many students to take advantage of all scholarship opportunities; however, even if students combed all scholarship sources, there would still not be enough scholarship aid for all capable students with financial need.

This is a repeat remark: if there is need and you have a good record, you will enhance your chances by applying to less-competitive schools. These schools are eager to add competent, bright students to their student population and will be far more liberal in awarding financial assistance than the competitive schools. One year students in our school secured a total of more than $200,000 in scholarship aid, and if some of the needy students in this graduating class had been willing to lower their sights, this amount could easily have been higher.

Unless you are an athlete, for the most competitive or prestige schools, you must have a superior record plus excellent test scores. In addition, you must show financial need and must convince the admissions committee that you are the type of person, in both extracurricular activities and personality make-up, that they would be pleased to have on their campus. With all of this, there are no assurances, because there are many, many students who fill this bill, and the amount of aid is limited.

For most colleges, you should be able to offer averages of C+ or better, good College Boards or ACT scores, and evidence of financial need. With some schools, the greater emphasis may be placed on class rank and a lesser amount on test scores. The extent of variations can only be given to you by your guidance counselors, and even they must be cautious as they attempt to predict what a college will do with scholarship applications. The major complication in making a prediction is the fact that counselors have no way of determining in advance how many other capable students will be applying for scholarships. If there is less competition, chances for scholarship help are improved; if there are comparable or better candidates, opportunities diminish.

Some colleges will offer blanket scholarship help to students graduating in the upper third, upper fourth, upper sixth, or upper tenth of the graduating class. Their offers vary from grants-in-aid of $100 to half or full tuition. This information may be secured by checking the college bulletins which come into the guidance office every year at different intervals. This will necessitate your returning periodically to see if any more recent information is available.

HELPFUL SCHOLARSHIP SOURCES

Trained counselors will inform you that it is utterly impossible for them to help you find out about *all* scholarship sources. To this day, no one has published a complete guide on scholarships, and even if a source book did come out tomorrow, it would become outdated in a very short period of time. There are, however, some sources that can give you good information of available financial aid. Some of these are:

American Legion, Committee on Education and Scholarships. *Need a Lift? Educational Opportunities.* Indianapolis: National Child Welfare Division of the American Legion. (Revised annually)

Chronicle Guidance Publications. *Student Aid Annual—Student Aid Bulletins.* Moravia, New York. (Published annually)

Chronicle Guidance Publications. *Scholarships, Loans, and Awards Offered by Independent and AFL-CIO Affiliated Labor Unions.* Moravia, New York. (Published annually)

Chronicle Guidance Publications. *Scholarships, Loans, and Awards Offered by the Fifth States, District of Columbia, and Puerto Rico.* Moravia, New York. (Published annually)

College Entrance Examination Board. *Meeting College Costs: A Guide for Parents and Students.* Princeton, New Jersey. (Revised periodically)

College Entrance Examination Board. *The Official College Entrance Examination Board Guide to Financial Aid for Students and Parents.* New York: Simon & Schuster, Inc. (1975)

Cox, Claire. *How to Beat the High Cost of College.* New York: Dial Press. (1971)

Feingold, Norman S. *Scholarships, Fellowships, and Loans.* Cambridge, Mass.: Bellman Publishing Co. (Vol. V, 1973)

Keeslar, Oreon. *Financial Aids for Higher Education.* Dubuque, Iowa: Wm. C. Brown, Publisher. (Revised periodically)

Mathies, L., and E. Dixon, eds. *Scholarships, Fellowships, Grants, and Loans.* Riverside, New Jersey: Macmillan Publishing. (1974)

Proia, N., and V. Di Gaspari. *Barron's Handbook of American College Financial Aid.* Woodbury, New York: Barron's Educational Series. (1974)

Searing, Louis T., and Joyce W. Searing. *Student Financial Help: A Guide to Money for College.* Garden City, New York: Doubleday & Co. (1974)

Splaver, Sarah. *Your College Education: How to Pay for It.* New York: Simon & Schuster, Inc., Messner Division.

Suchar, Elizabeth W. *The Official College Entrance Examination Board Guide to Financial Aid for Students and Parents.* New York: Simon & Schuster, Inc.

Students are particularly advised to explore the Chronicle Guidance Bulletins, since these are revised periodically and are probably the most up-to-date literature with comprehensive coverage of scholarship sources. *Scholarships, Fellowships, and Loans,* a publication of the Bellman Publishing Company, and the American Legion material, also have proven helpful to needy students.

Students should also read carefully posters received by their school describing the latest scholarship offers of different colleges. You would naturally check the catalogs of the colleges of your choice, then write to these colleges for scholarship blanks and special bulletins.

Your guidance office may offer you some or all of the following excellent aids: the source and reference materials mentioned above, periodic late reports on new scholarships as reported in Lovejoy's *College Guide Digest,* posters and announcements received from colleges or scholarship sponsors, cards and files listing scholarship opportunities, and rosters of graduates and the types of scholarships received. These materials, plus personal information available to your counselors, are yours for the asking. All that is required is a visit to the guidance office, a request for scholarship data, and relinquishing some of your time for a check of the literature.

NEWSPAPER ANNOUNCEMENTS

We are no longer surprised by some of the unusual scholarships that are picked up by some of our students. We can recall one young lady winning a $500 award for writing an essay on the importance of the trucking industry, and a young man won a trip to Mexico and $1,000 toward tuition for an essay written on another unusual topic. Both these students gathered their information about the scholarships from the newspapers.

You will notice, as you read newspapers, that there are announcements about the standard scholarships, the national programs, the NROTC, and Coast Guard Academies; occasionally you may find information that never appears in guidance offices. If you are resourceful and ambitious, you should not overlook this method of gaining information beyond that offered in books, brochures, or in your guidance office.

LOCAL SERVICE CLUBS

In every community there are Boosters Clubs and such organizations as the Lions, Kiwanis, Rotary, and Elks. Some of these organizations contribute to national scholarship programs and conduct financial aid programs of their own. Quite often these service organizations make contributions covering tuition or part of a needy student's college expenses. Do not overlook these groups for possible help.

Within communities there are often foundations (public and private) which rarely publicize their services. If you have information about the existence of a local or special foundation, be certain to write for literature and submit an application blank at a sufficiently early date. Too often, such foundations are oversubscribed, and when their funds are depleted, they discontinue grants for the year.

As you can see, it is extremely difficult to locate all the available scholarship sources. We have mentioned the need for a comprehensive guide covering all of these aids, but it seems unlikely that this will be forthcoming in the near future.

All of this leads to one point. If you need and want help, explore all possible sources, show initiative, be willing to ask questions, read material, and write for help. Over the last few years we have been pleasantly surprised by the ability of some of our students to win scholarships. We have found others who spoke about need and actually *were* in poor financial circumstances, but lacked that little extra drive to explore and exhaust all avenues that might lead to assistance.

PART-TIME EMPLOYMENT IN COLLEGE

Almost all college catalogs contain information about their placement office and job services. Some indicate job opportunities within the school as well as in the surrounding community. Some suggest that, if you are counting on employment to defray your expenses, you consider delaying part-time employment until after your first year in college. They base this suggestion on the problems encountered by many freshmen in adjusting to the academic demands of college.

Some of the schools make arrangements, at the time you apply for scholarship help, to give job awards which they may discuss with you prior to your entrance into college; some even recommend that you explore this problem with them at the end of your high school senior year. If you are eager to secure this type of help, be certain to notify the college as early as possible and request information about employment opportunities. If you visit the college and have an interview, ask your interviewer if it would be possible to discuss employment opportunities with the school's placement officials.

Don't overlook the College Work-Study Program if you have need and *must* earn part of your educational expenses. If you qualify for this program, your Financial Aid officer will assist in placing you.

ALLOCATING TIME FOR WORK

An issue confronting college freshmen holding part-time employment is the question of their ability to work without interfering with school performance. If a school recommends that you delay accepting employment, you should respect its judgment unless you are unusually gifted and absorb school work with ease. For the first year of college, you might find it more feasible to depend on summer or holiday employment rather than a regular job which will take away much time from your school work.

If you feel obligated to work during the school year, be ready to recognize the difficulty of coping with both work and school. If you discover that your work is affecting your studies, you would be wise to search for other sources of financial help.

A request to a college for financial assistance will result in your receiving a brochure with detailed coverage of the institution's involvement in the many financial aid programs. Don't overlook any of these sources, and don't be hesitant about going into debt for an education. Most students would not object to buying a new sports car on an installment plan. The life of a car would rarely extend beyond five or six years, but an education will be with you for the rest of your life. Money borrowed for an education will eventually be regained and repaid many times over.

CHAPTER 9

ADJUSTING TO COLLEGE

Getting into college is one problem—staying in and doing well academically is another. Learning how to make social adjustments in new situations is still a third problem.

Statistics on the drop-out rate in college show that from 33 1/3 percent to 40 percent of those who go to college fail to graduate. Some have to leave for financial reasons; others leave for such personal reasons as marriage and family problems; still a few others find that college was never suitable for them. A percentage become disenchanted with the curriculum, but most who leave do so because of academic difficulties which are frequently interrelated with other problems of adjustment.

For many students, college is their first experience away from home without parental supervision, and some find it difficult to acquire the necessary self-discipline. Many high schools and teachers have spoon-fed their students; as a result, some college freshmen may find it difficult to learn to fend for themselves when given unsupervised assignments. Many learning situations in high school call for rote memorization, and the transition in college to the demand for individual reasoning is difficult.

College students away from home for the first time will often be disturbed to find a new type of "freedom" in their college environment. They may be exposed to problems of gambling, drinking, and the use of marijuana or drugs to a far greater degree than ever before, and the results can be unfortunate. Extracurricular activities, athletics, and social events may prove so inviting that studies will be neglected.

These are some of the problems you may face, and the sooner you become realistic about them, the better your chances for survival in college.

One suggestion we can make is that on your visits to colleges you speak to some of the students about typical problems. Recent graduates also might relate to you some of their experiences and problems. These talks might give you a better perspective of the minor problems and major issues that will confront you.

FRATERNITIES AND SORORITIES

A few years ago this issue rightfully would have been considered one of the major decisions you would have to make in college. The problem has diminished somewhat, since most fraternities and sororities have discontinued hazing and have substituted worthwhile projects for pledgees. At one time almost all social clubs were restrictive both as to race and religion, but such practices are being discarded rapidly.

The decision to join a fraternity or sorority is still one that must be given some thought. The advantages of these groups are that they provide training in getting along with people, they offer social and cultural opportunities for students, they offer a pleasant place to live, and they give one friendship and a feeling of camaraderie. Indeed, some people consider fraternities and sororities extremely helpful, since these organizations pride themselves on their successes and will help their fellow members in times of academic stress.

Others resent fraternities because of their restrictive nature and failure to pledge all students. There are objections to the stranglehold some of the fraternities have on school offices and resentment of the patronizing attitude of the members of certain Greek letter organizations. Consideration of joining should take into account the additional cost of living in a fraternity or sorority house, the time demands of keeping up with the social standards of your fellow-members, and the need to compete financially with your fellow "Greeks."

If these organizations are disturbing to you, avoid campus situations where most students join. Look for the college that has no such organizations or where fewer than 30 percent of the student body hold membership. In a college where the atmosphere is permeated with fraternity and sorority life and activities, you can only add to your unhappiness. Failure to be pledged or rejection for membership is not a pleasant experience.

Conversations with former students have disclosed that those who were active in fraternities and sororities were impressed by their programs and highly recommended them. Other students who did not join these organizations contended that life went on comfortably without them, and, given the opportunity, they would relive their college lives without joining.

ACADEMIC DIFFICULTIES

In the book *College Freshmen Speak Out,* Agatha Townsend lists reactions of college freshmen to their experiences. Among the comments are criticism of secondary schools because of their failure to prepare students for college academic life. (This may have merit in some cases but is used by many students to place the blame on others rather than on themselves, where it probably belongs.) Some deplored their lack of writing experience; others were highly critical of their inability to use library resource materials; many found it difficult to budget their time with the reduced class time and the proportionate increase in assignments.

You should also realize that the academic level in most colleges will be higher than it was in your secondary school. For example, the college that admits you may accept only those in the upper half of your high school class. As a result, you will be competing with many more students on your own level or with more ability than you have. This may mean a lowering of your average and if you are a marginal student, possible failure.

The size and scope of assignments distributed by college professors and the number of books you are expected to read may come as a shock. You will also have to adapt yourself to taking midterm and final examinations instead of the daily quizzes and weekly or cycle tests that you had in high school.

These are some of the problems you will be facing when you enter college. None are insurmountable. Although your secondary school might help you by conducting one or two college-type courses, you could do a far better job of helping yourself by increasing your outside reading, doing extra assignments, budgeting your time, expending more effort, and doing better research on term papers.

OTHER PROBLEMS

Some students attending college for the first time become homesick, and a few of these must leave school for this reason. If you anticipate having this problem, getting away from home at different times for varying periods long before you enter college may be good preventive medicine. This may not resolve the entire problem but may partially condition you to being on your own. Making friends, participating in activities, and having things to do should also ease your adjustment.

A college offers innumerable activities, and you will have to use judgment in joining clubs and offering your services to various organizations. You may have to learn moderation; remember that studying and achieving an education should be your major objective in attending college. Extracurricular activities, important as they are, should be placed in their proper perspective. This is not intended to minimize the importance of activities which may help develop hidden talents, bring out leadership qualities, and assist in the modification of personality traits.

Dating is important, but you may have to learn how to restrict the number of dates you make or accept. You must learn how to forego immediate pleasures by first setting aside the proper amount of time for studying or preparing papers.

The problem of budgeting your money may be a new experience for you. If you receive an allowance at the beginning of the month and spend your money unwisely, you may find yourself without funds for one, two, or three weeks. As much as your parents like to hear from you, the appeal for funds does not strike a pleasant chord.

Card playing and gambling go on at most colleges, and the temptation to join in this activity is always great. The unfortunate thing about card playing is not merely the possible loss of money, but the excessive amount of time devoted to it, with grades suffering as a consequence.

It disturbs us to have to raise some of these problems, but many students have never given them a thought, and others seem to ignore them. They are real problems, and you would be wise to decide how to deal with them without any loss of academic or social status.

COLLEGE SERVICES AND AIDS

Being away from home, at times you will have need for help from more mature persons. If you have religious affiliations, you should naturally seek out the related organizations within your school. Actually, it is one of the considerations you should keep in mind when selecting a college. *Lovejoy's College Guide* and Cass and Birnbaum's *Comparative Guide to American Colleges* have a listing of such organizations for the principal religions at different schools. College catalogs also contain information about these groups or the presence of representatives of different denominations at the school.

Your residence hall may have a counselor, house mother, or graduate student; these individuals have been placed in their positions to help you with your personal problems. Use them without hesitation. Your college may also offer counseling services and may have a clinic with trained social workers, psychologists, and psychiatrists.

If you are beset by problems and are running into difficulty in making an adjustment in college, do not overlook these possible sources of help.

TRANSFERRING FROM ONE
COLLEGE TO ANOTHER

Almost without fail, at the conclusion of the freshmen year at college a number of students transfer to different institutions. The percentage grows smaller in the circles of the more selective schools, but the problem is still a universal one. The necessity of transfer often is brought about by a student's failure to check out the social climate or to explore degree requirements of the school he selected.

Some transfers occur because of change of plans and the inability of a college to accommodate the shift in career requirements. Dissatisfaction because of failure to develop a good social life or make friends is another reason some students change schools. The difficulty of competing in certain academic situations also contributes to a need for transfers.

Viewing a transfer with alarm is completely unnecessary. In many cases, there are valid and worthwhile reasons for effecting transfers. In other situations a transfer may help solve a personal problem and improve a student's adjustment. It is not unusual for individuals to err in their original college selections. If you fall into this category, you should be willing to recognize and rectify your mistakes. Executing a transfer with good judgment and proper deliberation may help you to attain a better education.

Many students do not discuss the issue of transfer with their school officials in the mistaken belief that such a decision should be carried out in secrecy. Without question, college officials are interested in your welfare and will gladly assist you in any way they can. In some cases, an interview with a school counselor might lead to your continued stay at the school. This could benefit you in your adjustment, as you would thus avoid taking the easy way out of escaping to another setting. It might also save you loss of credits and time.

College counselors or officers can assist you in a positive manner with your plans. Knowing you, having your record, and being acquainted with your problem, they may give you excellent advice on the selection of another school or the resolution of your dilemma.

There appears to be an increase in the available space for transfers, with possible the exception of major state universities and prestigious colleges. In part, this may be attributed to students taking time out to "find themselves" or their questioning the limited job opportunities if they do obtain a diploma. All of this will make it easier to effect a change if transfer becomes inevitable. As soon as you have made the decision, and it has been approved by your present college officials and your family, you must decide on alternate schools. Planning for the selection of a college for transfer should duplicate almost step-by-step the same considerations you gave, or should have given, to your original selection of a college.

Once you have narrowed down your choices, you should immediately send letters to the Registrars or the Directors of Admission of the colleges you have chosen. These letters might review your present circumstances, including the name of the school you are attending, subjects and units completed, your most recent grades, and your reasons for desiring a transfer. This type of letter could be considered a preliminary application and should result in a response indicating no interest, some interest, or the possibility of acceptance. Some individuals might prefer sending a brief note, with an expressed interest in transferring to a particular program and requesting to know if the college expects to have space. If schools demand special tests, notify them when you took the tests and offer to forward scores with your application. When you receive the application blank, fill it out properly and forward any needed high school and college transcripts. Carefully check the special requirements of the school and satisfy them as soon as you submit an official application. Visits and interviews with the admissions office may be expected, and you should unhesitatingly make an appointment and arrange for a visit. Remember that you are investing money and time; a few extra hours, coupled with mature deliberation, may result in more favorable placement for you.

CHAPTER 10

CHOOSING A CAREER

Going back to our previous discussion of a liberal arts education as distinguished from attendance at a specialized school, we return to an important problem—that of choosing a career. Ideally, you would decide on a career area in the 7th or 8th grade, plan your high school program accordingly, and then work out a suitable college program. There are a few students who make their decisions early in life and follow through for at least one or two years of college; however, even among these, there are many who change their minds.

You may recall in our discussion of engineering that we mentioned the vast number of students who move to other fields. This shifting of careers and plans also takes place in the premedical, scientific, and many other fields. If you are undecided about a career, a liberal arts course will give you ample opportunity to do exploratory work through different subject experiences in your first two years at college. If you are disturbed about your indecision, we can only assure you that many of your friends are in the same position. We can also tell you that as long as you are aware of the need for making a decision at some date and are giving consideration to the problem, you are moving in the right direction.

METHODS OF SELECTING A CAREER

Aids available to high school students in making career choices vary from a single session of a few minutes with an administrative official to a series of counseling sessions over a period of years with one counselor and possible subjection to an all-inclusive battery of tests.

Most schools today make provisions for all students to write vocational essays once or twice during high school. Many schools invite guest speakers for career conferences or career day programs to enlighten young people about professions or jobs. Some schools have film libraries and other audio-visual materials that may be used throughout the school year. Many school systems make available such courses as "Occupational Self-Appraisal," "Occupations," and "Human Relations," which devote a great deal of time to the problem of selecting a career. Some have developed their own testing programs or have contacts with outside agencies.

OCCUPATIONAL LITERATURE

With increased specialization and the development of new occupations in recent years, there has been a corresponding increase in descriptive occupational literature in the form of books, brochures, pamphlets, and one-page sheets. Most libraries today contain sections that are completely devoted to this type of literature, and practically all guidance offices and school libraries have space set aside for material dealing with occupations.

Good literature which follows the outline established by the National Vocational Guidance Association will feature job descriptions, related job areas, skills and aptitudes that are required, necessary training or education, and other important aspects of an occupation. You should use this literature even if you are reading about jobs in which you have little or no interest. It is helpful because it gives you a framework for considering other occupations and supplies knowledge about occupations you might normally never consider. Additionally, it may help to make you aware of the many new vocations that are appearing constantly.

The publisher of this book, Vocational Guidance Manuals, has specialized for years in preparing comprehensive well-rated career books. If you write to them at 620 South Fifth Street, Louisville, Kentucky 40202, they would be happy to mail you a list of their publications and price lists.

There are many other publishers whose literature would also merit your attention. Check your local library and school guidance office to see what kinds of career materials they have available.

EXPERIENCES

Experiences in your subject areas should also prove helpful in giving insight into your own abilities and may act as predictors of possible future success in certain fields. Part-time and summer employment will also afford you an opportunity to become acquainted with job areas and may give you a realistic picture of what is entailed in certain positions. Hobbies and extracurricular activities are additional facets for exploring your adaptability to different occupations.

Some students are asked to write a vocational essay based on occupational literature and interviews with those who have on-the-job experience. Even though your school may not ask you to do this, you should be willing to give up some time to making contacts of this type outside of school and to interviewing a number of people to help you obtain a better picture of the career you have chosen.

TESTING PROGRAMS IN THE HIGH SCHOOL

Today most high schools have developed testing programs to help you with your career plans. You may take intelligence tests, reading tests, achievement tests in a number of areas, interest tests, and a battery of aptitude tests. Test results generally are placed in your cumulative folder and are used in discussions with you and your parents about your future. Additionally, you may be given profile sheets and notices of explanation about the meaning and significance of test results. Used wisely by the school for counseling purposes, these may help you considerably in making career decisions.

WHEN TO CONSIDER ADDITIONAL TESTING

If your high school testing and counseling program is inadequate, or if you have problems that are peculiar to you, you might consider outside testing, with the approval of your guidance department. The issue is raised here because so many people assume that testing will resolve their problem of a career decision. Tests have limitations and must always be interpreted only as indicators of potential abilities.

If you are not doing well in school, tests have the possible advantage of spotting your weaknesses so that you may be placed in remedial programs. Such tests might also indicate that you have academic potential without any obvious deficiencies; then your problem would be one of trying to find out why you are not working up to your level of ability. Tests that show possible success in the engineering field will not do the work for you; nor will the favorable test results, minus an appropriate academic record, enable you to enter or succeed at an engineering college.

Consider additional testing at the recommendation of individuals who know you and are qualified to make this suggestion. If you do make arrangements for special testing, do not expect the tests to be a remedy for all your difficulties.

BONA-FIDE TESTING AGENCIES AND RESOURCES

With the continued development and expanded use of tests, you will find a number of testing agencies making their appearance in your locale. If these agencies advertise their services publicly, you should automatically recognize that they are not members of any of the professional groups. All professional organizations and associations prohibit their members from soliciting clients by advertising. There are well-organized and certified testing services and agencies, college or university counseling clinics, and highly qualified vocational counselors and counseling psychologists. These are the only ones that you should consider using.

If you are fortunate enough to be located near accredited agencies that have these services, contact them without hesitation. Otherwise write to the International Association of Counseling Services, 1607 New Hampshire Avenue N.W., Washington, D.C. 20009 for a list of approved counseling agencies in your district. You may also secure this information from your guidance office, your local Personnel and Guidance Association, or your State Psychological Association.

Remember that charlatans do exist and are plying their trade. As long as you are willing to spend money for counseling or testing services, you might as well receive the benefit of the services of completely accredited testing agencies or properly certified individuals.

GUIDANCE SERVICES IN COLLEGES

One of the major trends in the guidance movement has been the spread of guidance services from high school down to the junior high and elementary school, and up through junior college and college. A number of colleges now offer pre-orientation counseling and guidance clinics during the summer for high school juniors. These services, generally conducted on a professional level, might prove worthwhile if your school system has a limited guidance program. If you desire this help, request names of schools from your guidance staff.

Many colleges arrange now for a special orientation program for entering freshmen, allocating from two days to a full week for testing, lectures, and other aids in selecting curriculum and career. Colleges also have expanded their counseling services; and you most likely will have one counselor, or the services of a group of counselors, throughout your days in college. Added to this will be the career programs now spreading throughout colleges, the talks by employers during your college days, and finally, the visits by placement officers during your senior year. So you can see, even if you have not decided on a career in high school, help will be available to you at a later date.

CHAPTER 11

LOOKING AHEAD

In 1960, there were about 1 million college entrants; in September, 1965, over 1½ million students entered college. The total enrollment of first-time students in institutions of higher education (two-year public and private, four-year public and private, and universities) rose to well over 2 million by the fall of 1972. In the past few years enrollment figures have varied, a situation brought about by some interesting facts which bear investigation:

• College enrollments are not dropping because of a diminishing number of college-age youths. According to Census Bureau data, the number of college-age youths will increase until 1980. Prohibitive costs and the unwillingness of states to fund higher education in proportion to inflation rates may be greater factors in the drop in enrollment.

• The rate of college attendance of the 18- to 21-year-old group and of high school graduates does not remain stable.

• Enrollments in colleges and universities are not equally affected by the national change in college attendance. Despite a nationwide increase of 3.9 percent between 1972 and 1973, some states experienced declines in enrollment.

• There are numerous predictions that the current instability in enrollment will be with us for a number of years.

• There will be problems of funding higher education for many years to come.

Between 1965 and 1970, colleges had as many as 40,000 vacancies, and this was during a time of supposedly tight admissions. Today there are figures of far more than 150,000 vacancies per year, and this does not even take into consideration the closing of a number of private schools and, believe it or not, the expectation of closing some state schools with decreased freshman enrollments. Stated in another fashion, outside of some state schools and the very select institutions, we are now in a buyer's market.

IMPROVED COUNSELING

Counselors today are far more sophisticated and knowledgeable than their counterparts of ten years ago. Because of such factors as the Conant Report, with its recommendation of one counselor for every 250 students, and the National Defense Education Act, with its provisions for training guidance personnel, there has been an increase in counseling services, both in quantity and quality. The implication for the college aspirant and his parents is the promise of more, and undoubtedly better, assistance. More and more school systems have now arranged to have their counselors visit schools in different parts of the country, thus helping direct high school graduates to good schools rarely considered in the past by college applicants. More schools are participating in the activities of the Association of College Admission Counselors, thus enabling counselors to meet many college representatives from different sections of the country.

College guidance in secondary schools is also improving through the expansion of services and the increase in the number of directories providing profiles of colleges of every type and level.

Looking over my book shelves, I see the following: *Summary of Colleges Interested in Additional Applicants* by Chronicle Guidance; The College Entrance Examination Board's *The College Handbook; College Admissions Data Service,* published by Educational Research Data; articles from *Changing Times* on "Colleges with Room for More Students" and "The College Blue Books"; and Cass and Birnbaum's *Comparative Guide to American Colleges.* The latter, which offers interesting vignettes emphasizing the social setting, academic climate, etc. of many colleges, has been the forerunner of a welcome approach to the problem of college selection. All of the aforementioned aids, added to the many books and directories listed in the recommended reading list at the end of this book, provide counselors and students with unlimited assistance.

If you are living in a community with well-trained counselors who have access to the many available excellent aids, your problems pertaining to college selection can be eased. If your community does not offer these services, you may have to consider outside help or insist that your school system incorporate an acceptable guidance program.

COLLEGE SERVICES

With the availability of space, colleges ranging from the most selective to the unaccredited are expanding their visits to schools. Representatives speak to students and staff; some of them organize evening meetings for students and parents. A few colleges (Midwest College Council, Finger Lakes Colleges, Union of Independent Colleges of Art, etc.) have banded together to apprise students of their offerings. Several groups of colleges, such as "College Bound" and "College Admissions" are visiting different areas; announcements of date, time, and locale appear in local newspapers and are made available through posters issued

Junior colleges, community colleges, and technical institutes have shown remarkable growth in recent years, attracting those interested in employment in paraprofessional, technical, and skilled positions. The students above are receiving special instruction in horticulture and greenhouse operation.

through local secondary schools. A growing number of institutions with limited staff periodically send representatives who stay in hotels in large cities; these admissions counselors are available for interviews by appointment.

To aid students and counselors, many colleges are issuing more precise brochures and profiles describing their schools. A number of colleges have forwarded filmstrips and an accompanying phonograph record to supply us with a pictorial and verbal picture of their school.

All of this adds up to improved counseling of students.

COMMUNITY AND JUNIOR COLLEGES

One of the interesting aspects of the college admissions picture is the increase in the number of community and junior colleges which, in over thirty states, make up about one-third of all collegiate institutions and enroll more than 2,700,000 students. California alone has over 93 junior colleges, Florida has more than 28, New Jersey has 19, and other states have been rapidly adding to their community college programs. The growth of public, two-year colleges has been phenomenal. There are now over 1,000 junior colleges, about 800 of which are public institutions; 155 are church related; and approximately 80 are independent. Many of these schools have regional accreditation and are becoming springboards toward higher degrees.

Community and junior colleges are quickly becoming reliable sources of needed workers in paraprofessional, technical, and skilled occupations. Illustrative of the programs that may be taken at two-year colleges are the following: accounting technology, advertising design, communications and broadcasting technology, banking, insurance and real estate, fashion illustration, interior design, transportation technology, computer programming technology, animal laboratory assistant, cytotechnology, dental assistant, dental hygiene, medical laboratory assistant, optometric assistant, inhalation therapy, automotive technology, chemical technology, construction and building technology, drafting and design, ornamental horticulture, legal assistant, and library assistant.

The best source of the varied courses is *American Junior Colleges,* published by the American Council on Education and revised approximately every four years. Chronicle Guidance's *Guide to Two-Year College Majors and Careers* also is very helpful.

A LOOK AT THE FUTURE

With the available space in colleges, students and parents can breathe more easily and counselors will have more time to do counseling and be more effective in tailoring their post-high school placement. The bright spots on the college admissions horizon include the following:

- Ample space, with many more choices available.
- Better trained, more sophisticated, and more knowledgeable counselors.
- Development of services (profiles, manuals, and guides) to assist counselors, students, and parents.
- Improvement in college services relating to admissions.
- Less emphasis on test scores, with a stronger weighting of academic records.
- Greater use of college facilities, with weekend college programs and the attraction of many more mature individuals to colleges on a part-time basis.
- The fantastic growth and popularity of community and junior colleges.
- More stable federal scholarship aid and loan programs.
- Greater selectivity of professors, with the glutted market of Ph.D.'s.
- Concentrated thrust into more practical curricula, as well as an increase in cooperative education.

Despite the above, colleges still have many problems. Money is not available for the funding of science laboratories, specialized equipment, and building construction to accommodate larger enrollments. There is far from enough scholarship aid to take care of the needs of the lower-middle and middle-middle class applicants. Class sizes are increasing in order to keep down the operating costs. More and more schools are arranging for many lecture courses, with class size as high as 500, and some are giving courses via TV. There has been and apparently will continue to be a steady increase in tuition rates, placing more of the burden of educating the populace on the shoulders of community and state institutions. The latter are now feeling the economic crunch and may have to become more selective.

I noticed not too long ago that a state school had turned down a student whom they would have accepted without any hesitation a year ago. One state university which was willing to consider non-resident students in the top half of their graduating classes is now limiting its out-of-state entrants to those in the top quarter. Another state institution, which a few years ago accepted students ranked in the top 2/3 of their graduating classes, will now not consider anyone below the top 10 percent. Another state university which was willing to accept any honor student is now insisting upon those with superhonor grades, plus exceptional test scores. To further confuse the picture, there are some state institutions which are practically offering open admissions to students outside their own areas.

Another problem is the definite movement to graduate training, with the concomitant fight for space. In the near future, this also will create congestion in the labor market. By way of illustration, two out of every three law graduates are having difficulty securing placement in their own field.

At one time counselors concentrated all their attention on just finding a spot in college for the aspiring student. Now that admissions are easier, they have other problems—with funding of education and, interestingly enough, the possibility of over-training a percentage of our population. During the next few years, a number of small private colleges and possibly a few state institutions will be forced to close their doors. Community colleges will probably continue to enroll large numbers of students, as increased emphasis is placed on career training, particularly in para-professional areas.

CHAPTER 12

SUMMARY AND TIMETABLE

EIGHTH GRADE

- Watch for and take part in discussions at school about your future plans and high school course selections.
- Bring home all information and have your parents join you in your deliberations.
- Parents should visit schools and attend all meetings arranged to assist students with their decisions.
- If your school expects you to do a paper on your future career, do so wholeheartedly. It will help you more than it will the teacher.
- Start looking through college catalogs for a general picture of units required for admission. *The College Handbook,* published by the CEEB, will give you concisely the requirements of schools that are rated by many as being extremely selective. If you are having difficulties with specific subjects, you might check admission requirements at junior college, two-year technical institutes, colleges of business administration, state (teachers) colleges, etc. Securing a picture of varying requirements may help you plan your high school program wisely.
- Work out your final plans for high school with your teachers or counselors. Their suggestions and advice should merit your respect and agreement.

NINTH GRADE (Freshman Year)

• Attack your schoolwork with vigor and develop a good routine of studying that will apply to your approach to all of your assignments. Do not make empty promises about commencing tomorrow or the next day.

• Read for pleasure and also to expand your vocabulary. Pay attention to your mathematics fundamentals. A steady application in these areas will be far more helpful in preparing for college boards than all the review books and coaching schools put together.

• Evaluate yourself in relation to your adaptation to subjects, and be ready to modify or change your curriculum.

• If specialized tests are offered at your school, take them. Test-taking experiences should result in relaxing you for the many tests to which you will be exposed at a later date.

• Continue reading occupational literature and school catalogs.

• Take advantage of opportunities to participate in extracurricular activities. Try many with the understanding that you will eventually select those that seem suitable and have more meaning to you.

TENTH GRADE (Sophomore Year)

• STUDY—AND READ!

• Narrow down your extracurricular activities so that you may develop depth in a few areas.

• Recheck your subject selection with your counselor on the basis of continued reading of college catalogs.

• If your grades are good and there is financial need, begin looking at scholarship information.

• Consider taking Achievement Tests if you have completed a subject (i.e., biology).

ELEVENTH GRADE (Junior Year)

• Apply yourself seriously to the problem of selection of a college.

• Using criteria listed in this book, start to narrow your choices down to 10 or 12 colleges (fewer if possible).

• If the NMSQT/PSAT's are given in October at your school, be certain to register for them.

• Begin looking at the list of colleges that invite applications for Early Acceptance.

• Consider taking the practice College Boards or ACT's in the winter or spring. Remember to check the specific demands of all the colleges you are considering. If even one asks for the SAT/Achievement Tests or ACT's, be certain to take them. In line with the requests of Early Acceptance schools, take your SAT/Achievemen Tests or ACT's at the times suggested by them.

• Be certain to attend as many college, school, and career conferences as you can.

• Be on the alert for college announcements of visitation days and take advantage of those within a few hours' drive of your home.

• Go over the family budget to determine the financial aspects of your proposed education.

• Continue narrowing down your choice of schools.

• Plan your visits, which should start toward the close of this year; be certain to send letters with the date and time of your arrival.

• Toward the end of the academic year you should write for application blanks and scholarship information.

ᴅiligently look through the basic sources on scholarships.
● If you expect to apply for Early Acceptance, arrange to forward your SAT or ACT scores and start preparing your application.

TWELFTH GRADE (Senior Year)

● Those planning on Early Acceptance should be certain to file applications and have their school forward transcripts and other necessary papers in September or no later than October 31.
● Continue to check through catalogs, to attend college, school and career conferences, and to review scholarship literature in the guidance office and library.
● Narrow your choice of colleges down to three or four and secure your counselor's approval of your final selections. If you have aspirations for top level schools, consider applying to more than five to protect your interests.
● Prepare application blanks carefully.
● Check deadline dates for College Boards and ACT's, and file your applications on time.
● Send in your application blanks after the beginning of your senior year. Be certain that they are filed far in advance of any final date determined by the individual college.
● Prepare all scholarship blanks and the Parents' Confidential or Family Financial Statement if required by any schools.
● Sit back, wait patiently, and hope for acceptance at your first choice college.

FINAL NOTE

This book was not written to make students apprehensive about college admissions. The future is far from bleak. The problem of gaining admission to college is less acute than it was in years past, and the available evidence points to the fact that all applicants will be given an opportunity to continue their education beyond high school. The old saying, "There is a college for everybody," is very applicable these days.

There is a deceptiveness about the ease of placement, however. In times of easy college admissions, students tend to spend less time researching, exploring, and investigating to find exactly the right college. Consequently, many fail to apply to a school that will best serve their interests. Take time to consider and be very selective about the school you choose—evaluate your interests and abilities carefully and weigh them against the offerings of several different schools.

Beware of the assumption that a quality education can only be obtained at very selective colleges. Some very great businessmen, scholars, statesmen, and physicians were graduated from "non-brand name" schools. Additionally, most graduate and professional schools select students from a variety of schools—from the most selective to those with open admissions. For example, one top-rated medical school had 75 undergraduate colleges represented in its first-year class. Of the 75, approximately one-fourth were institutions that many students might easily have ignored as potential door-openers to accredited graduate and professional schools.

No matter what kind of school you attend after high school graduation—community college, junior college, or four-year college—remember that the amount of effort you expend in choosing the right one for you will pay dividends many times over in the future.

GOOD LUCK TO YOU!

APPENDIX A

GLOSSARY OF ABBREVIATIONS

ACH   Achievement Tests (Admissions Testing Program)
ACT   American College Testing Assessment
APA   American Psychological Association
APGA   American Personnel and Guidance Association
ATP   Admissions Testing Program
BEOG   Basic Educational Opportunity Grants
CEEB   College Entrance Examination Board
CSS   College Scholarship Service
CWSP   College Work-Study Program
EDP   Early Decision Plan
FFS   Family Financial Statement
GPA   Grade Point Average
NDSL   National Direct Student Loans
NMSC   National Merit Scholarship Corporation
PSAT/   Preliminary Scholastic Aptitude Test/
 NMSQT   National Merit Scholarship Qualifying Test
PCS   Parents' Confidential Statement
SAT   Scholastic Aptitude Test
SEOG   Supplemental Educational Opportunity Grants
SFS   Student Financial Statement
SNAS   Student Need Analysis Service

APPENDIX B

RECOMMENDED READING

American College Testing Program. *College Planning/Search Book.* Iowa City, Iowa: Author, 1975. (Updated periodically)

Barron's Educational Series. *Barron's Profiles of American Colleges,* 2 vols., 9th ed. Woodbury, New York: Barron's Educational Series, 1974. (Updated periodically)

Bird, Caroline. *The Case Against College.* New York: Bantam Books, 1975.

Cass, James, and Max Birnbaum. *Comparative Guide to American Colleges,* 7th ed. New York: Harper and Row, 1975. (Revised periodically)

Chronicle Guidance Publications, Inc. *Guide to External and Continuing Education.* Moravia, New York: Author, 1976.

____ . *Guide to Four-Year College Majors.* Moravia, New York: Author. (Published every year)

____ . *Guide to Two-Year College Majors and Careers.* Moravia, New York: Author. (Published every year)

____ . *Scholarships, Loans, and Awards Offered by the 50 States, D.C. and P.R.* Moravia, New York: Author. (Published every year)

____ . *Scholarships, Loans, and Awards Offered by Independent and AFL-CIO Affiliated Labor Unions.* Moravia, New York: Author (Published every year)

Directory Publishers Company. *College Programs for High School Students.* Hillsdale, New Jersey: Author. (Revised annually)

Furniss, W. Todd, ed. *American Universities and Colleges,* 11th ed. Washington, D.C.: American Council on Education, 1973. (Updated about every four years)

Gleazer, Edmond U., ed. *American Junior Colleges,* 8th ed. Washington, D.C.: American Council on Education, 1971. (New edition expected in the near future)

Hawes, Gene R., and Peter Novalis. *The New American Guide to Colleges,* 4th ed. New York City: Columbia University Press, 1972.

Keeslar, Oreon. *Financial Aids for Higher Education.* Dubuque, Iowa: William C. Brown. (Revised annually)

Lovejoy, Clarence E. *Lovejoy's College Guide.* New York City: Simon and Schuster, Inc., 1974. (Updated periodically)

U.S. Department of Labor. *Occupational Outlook Handbook,* 1976-77 edition. Washington, D.C.: 1976. (Generally revised every two years)

Watts, Susan F. *The College Handbook.* New York: College Entrance Examination Board, 1975. (Published approximately every three years)

APPENDIX C

OTHER SOURCES OF INFORMATION

**American College Testing
  Publications**
P.O. Box 168
Iowa City, Iowa 52240

**American Personnel and
  Guidance Association**
1607 New Hampshire Ave. N.W.
Washington, D.C. 20009

**American Psychological
  Association, Inc.**
1200 – 17th Street N.W.
Washington, D.C. 20036

**Association of College Admis-
  sions Counselors**
9933 Lawler Avenue, Suite
  500
Skokie, Illinois 60076

**College Board Admissions
  Testing Program**
Box 592-R
Princeton, N.J. 08540

**International Association of
  Counseling Services**
1607 New Hampshire Ave. N.W.
Washington, D.C. 20009

INDEX